C000171995

The Poetry Review

The Poetry Society, 22 Betterton Street, London WC2H 9BX

The Poetry Review

The Poetry Society, 22 Betterton Street, London WC2H 9BX
Tel: +44 (0)20 7420 9880 • Fax: +44 (0)20 7240 4818
Email: poetryreview@poetrysociety.org.uk
poetrysociety.org.uk/thepoetryreview

Editor: Emily Berry
Production: Michael Sims

ISBN: 978-1-911046-10-3 ISSN: 0032 2156
Cover artwork: Manshen Lo, manshenlo.com

. . .

SUBMISSIONS
For details of our submission guidelines,
please visit poetrysociety.org.uk/thepoetryreview

ADVERTISING
To place advertisements, visit
poetrysociety.org.uk/thepoetryreview or
contact Oliver Fox on +44 (0)20 7420 9886,
email: marketing@poetrysociety.org.uk

BOOKSHOP DISTRIBUTION
Central Books, 50 Freshwater Road, London
RM8 1RX, UK. Tel: +44 (0)20 8525 8800
or visit centralbooks.com

PBS OFFER TO POETRY SOCIETY MEMBERS
The Poetry Book Society offers Poetry Society
Members a special 10% discount (plus postage)
on books bought from poetrybooks.co.uk.
For details and to obtain the discount code,
please contact Paul McGrane on
+44 (0)20 7420 9881.

SUBSCRIPTIONS & SALES
UK individuals: £35 / Europe: £45
Rest of the World: £50 (overseas delivery by airmail)
Single issue: £8.95 plus postage. Order from
poetrysociety.org.uk/shop or contact Paul McGrane
on +44 (0)20 7420 9881. Pay by cheque
(sterling and US dollar cheques only),
credit card or Direct Debit.

The Poetry Review is also available on audio CD.

The Poetry Review is the magazine of
The Poetry Society and was first published in 1912.
A subscription to The Poetry Review is included as
part of membership of The Poetry Society. It is also
on sale in leading bookshops. A digital version of
the magazine is also available. Views expressed in
The Poetry Review are not necessarily those of The
Poetry Society; those of individual contributors
are not necessarily those of the Editor.

Charity Commission No. 303334.

Cover quote by Peter Gizzi, see p. 85

© The Poetry Review, The Poetry Society & contributors, 2018

THEPOETRYSOCIETY

CONTENTS

Report

Reviews

The Geoffrey Dearmer Prize 2017

EDITORIAL

I t's summer, so I'm thinking about the sea. I thought I might have
thought enough about the sea by now, but apparently not. *I must go
down to the seas again.* "Everything moves toward the sea", as Anzhelina
Polonskaya writes (in Andrew Wachtel's translation), in a poem of the
same title. Well, perhaps it's more the other way around, geologically
speaking. Or a back and forth, anyway. Some kind of power-play. The sea
is of course very powerful.

When I reread this issue's poetry, I noticed that "the sea is to be heard
all through it", which is what Virginia Woolf said in her diaries of *To the
Lighthouse.* Maybe I was particularly listening out for it. "[T]he sea's mouth
is louder now", writes Mel Pryor in 'Cliff', "than the spoken word". We
talk about the sea as if it is one thing. But the sea is not one thing, just as
language is not one thing – its iterations are infinite; "the sea's many
tongues" (Pryor again) have much to say, and – like poets, like people –
many different means of communicating.

In the discussions around translation in this summer's 'Enquiry'
section, Khairani Barokka, Sophie Collins and Carole Satyamurti consider
some of these different means, particularly those that are privileged over
others, and ask questions about the role of translation and of the translator
in a culture which still tends towards the drowning out of many of the
sea's tongues. Khairani Barokka notes, "Translation that may be a shared
sanctuary, a bridging to some, is an absence of this connectivity for others
[...]. The subject of which languages and poetries are chosen for translation,
and how they are translated, is always infused with biases."

For the hell of it, I looked up the symbolism of "sea" in an online dream dictionary, and was redirected to "ocean". But the ocean and the sea are not the same (though we do have an Ocean in this issue – Ocean Vuong, judge of the 2017 Geoffrey Dearmer Prize). The website Diffen, which "lets you compare anything", says under 'Ocean vs. Sea' that "oceans are vast bodies of water that cover roughly 70% of the earth. Seas are smaller and partially enclosed by land". Well, here we have some seas partially enclosed by poems. And a poem is another kind of way of comparing anything. In Rachael Allen's 'Promenade' and 'Remedies' – which among other things capture the melancholia of the (British) seaside town, its sense of thwarted possibilities – the sea might be like "openly wanting something", while in Iain Twiddy's 'The Needles' it's compared with the destructive forces of dementia – "the damage another night has brought in". Meanwhile, Ocean's chosen Dearmer winner, Raymond Antrobus, gives us a new poem in which the Mississippi River is compared with Ted Hughes (the Mississippi vs. Hughes...to find out who wins, turn to p. 134). There are also a number of rivers, by the way, in this issue – perhaps on their way to the sea?

Maybe if we lived in the water, poets would be drawn more to writing about one of the other elements. Maybe those wild deep-sea fish with see-through foreheads are always projecting their melancholia onto earth or something. In fluid dynamics, the branch of physics concerned with the motion of fluids, there is such a thing known as a 'wave of translation', a wave in which the water particles move forward with the form of the wave. What do I know about wave science? Not a thing, but I like the sound of this wave, which "does not stay where it is but travels to a distance" without losing a single droplet.

This year The Poetry Society is celebrating the twentieth anniversary of the Foyle Young Poets of the Year Award. The Poetry Review has published many former winners over the years, and by way of saying happy birthday this issue features poems by and/or reviews of several Foyle alumnae – A.K. Blakemore, Helen Mort and Phoebe Power, as well as a cameo by Chloe Stopa-Hunt (see pp. 131–32).

Emily Berry

HEATHER CHRISTLE

Thank you for all your help

When I came back
there was a new law.
It said don't touch anyone
and I obeyed it.
I had a great longing
to palm your blond head.
The closest we could get
was to hold a cardboard
box between us.
I held the north flap
and you held the east
and we stood there
for maybe one hour.
You said that was enough.
I do not love the law
but I have to love authority.
How could they not
know better than me?
I am one stalk of corn.
Very stupid.
I'd die without this
constant light and air.

When It's a Jar

When the cat leaves on the yellow quilt
a perfect muddy paw print
having gone out into the early wet morning
before there is even enough light
really to name it as such
it magnetises my whole sense of being
around it, as it's not the sort of event
or sight that often happens in my own life,
it seems to come from a picture or
not even that, it seems to come
from a book, almost as if the cat
were mocking me for my poor, unwritten
existence, people in books live the most
extraordinary lives and what's more
they are written by people who
– one has to imagine – have thoughts,
feelings, experiences even beyond what
they set into pages, and this is too much
for me to contemplate, that a person should
be capable not only of recording these
tiny immense observations of events such as
the cat casually requiring the "slovenly wilderness"
of the morning to surround the yellow quilt,
but also to have ideas about the history
of the word *calico* which in some places
brings to mind a small repetitive floral design
and in others a kind of sticky web
its sonic residue leaves on the tongue
and I stagger a little beneath the weight
of my awe for these people who
are so distinct from myself in that

whatever thoughts may come to me here
are set down in their entirety and stretched out
in a single flattened layer after which
my whole life and mind are left empty
like a flag with nary a symbol, a flag
I read – correctly – as one of glad surrender
to the burgeoning fullness of other people's lives.

RICHARD PRICE

I would like to meet people

I would like to meet people I have never met before.

I would like to meet my mother,
        as if she had lived beyond my twenty-third year.
'Twenty-something' is still a child of a kind,
        as I have learned from my own children.
Now that her sons were all leaving home
        she had just taken up painting again
so perhaps we could visit exhibitions together
               and both find new influences,
and she could tell me where she trained
and what the ideas about art were in those days,
and what was the argument her father had with the Army?

I'd tell my mother just enough about poetry not to put her off
and most of all we'd just laugh, and in the galleries she'd make that half-cough
    of hers
when she ventured into something risqué, or simply sensual.

I would like to meet my eldest child
as if she hadn't been born with catastrophic chromosomes.
We all need at least to try to accept our own shapes and dance patterns
        and the shapes and patterns of those around us:
yes, yes, we should all celebrate what there is to be celebrated – there is so
    much, even so –
but I do notice her exact contemporaries
        and admire their articulacy with a phone,
their breaking and making of friendships, their conspiracies,
and I know my daughter, who will always be approximately one in 'mental years',
would have loved to be among them.
Like them, she'd keep that certain distance from her father,
        who doesn't know anything about the real world.

I would like to meet the woman I called the love of my life,
a phrase which stands in severe reproach to me.
I used it in earnest when we were lovers
            but I failed the gravity of its declaration, merely heartfelt.
I am ashamed.
I would like to meet her as if the stroke which paralyses her to this day
            had not gripped her, suddenly, inexplicably,
                        a week before our seventh Feast of St Valentine.
In the years after, her illness tested me and I did not pass that test.

These days, sometimes, we help each other to visit exhibitions.
We navigate the frustrations of the 'modern transport network'.
These are well known to anyone dependent on the use of a wheelchair
                        but apparently hidden to everyone else.
We are still surprised together – did you know Duchamp was a sensitive
      portrait-maker,
or how soothing the target paintings of Jasper Johns can be?

I think of the mother I never knew, how she would have liked these
      gallery visits, too,
and, since there is visual skill in the family, I wonder if my daughter,
if she had not had distorted DNA, might have been an artist –
                        she might have liked to come along, too.
She, too, would want to know what was the argument her great grandfather
      had with the Army?

Too, too, too.

I would like to meet these people close to me who I have never met before,
though somehow while still being close to all the actual people I am lucky to
      know
who have been part-created by random acts of natural violence
            and by how, generally speaking, the world has treated them since;
by how, specifically speaking, I have treated them since.

Perhaps we would all travel more, separately, together, I don't know in
    what combinations
(managing two wheelchairs at one time is a task and a half,
              but we'd be helped comprehensively in this well-staffed daydream).
Beyond this almost useless geography
                  of longing and guilt and regret,
we'd meet 'real' people as if we were all real, too.

In the gentle tourism I imagine, not one of those we encountered
                would be a person we had met before,
and I bet almost everyone would like to hear my mother's explanation:
what was the argument her father had with the Army?

RACHAEL ALLEN

Promenade

Openly wanting something
like the opened-up lungs of a singer.
I walk by the carriage of the sea
and the vinegar wind assaults.
Is this an age of promise? I blush
to want. If I were walking around
with you, arm in arm, along some
iron promenade, you could fill me up
with chocolate, you could push back
my cuticles with want. I'll just lie down,
my ribs opened up in the old town square
and let the pigs root through my chest.

Desiccated Porcine Armour Thyroid

I am a gland, the smooth opal pearl
of a pig, who is bubbly with glands
the glands torn open in a pig's shorn neck
look like droplets of sperm
on the end of your glans
I eat the glands of pigs for breakfast
and I take a few in pills each night
slipping down my throat
a smooth oblong, like oysters or snot
I rub the loose, oily glands in my hands
to moisturise, pale mermaid's purses
salted like eyeballs, like lychees
and then I bathe in some glands
slipping around each other
as the miscreant lump under skin
a gland enlarged with the promise of sickness
grey and portentous
a gland cut open and placed within
another gland creates
a geode of glands
the colour of bad livers
the smell of bad lungs
full of poor white blood cells
or sometimes good white blood cells
or the blood work of a pig
whatever's farthest, most holy, to the ground

Remedies

Seek god's face in the pustule of a teenage girl
whose wrists smell like table sugar
whose hand you hold
under the green and white striped awning
of the beach café. Sand blows into ham sandwiches
while distemper accumulates at sea.
Green parsley and an excess of vitamins
we whisper remedies out of habit.
If we are passing through the water
and the water is delivering us from evil
forgiving us our trespasses, as we forgive
the cramping tide and waves
we might eventually enjoy grainy tea
in cardboard containers
and look forward to late at night
her arm stretched across me
pressing into my stomach and counting down
the space between waves
a best friend with green eyes
as shallow as a harbour pool.

MEL PRYOR

Night Watch with Stars and Considered Lilies

Are they stars or am I simply afflicted?
Every night ends, every night refuses to end

and the head feels heavy on its neck
like an illuminated globe
weighed down by seas, and land, and writing.

I rise and exit and under the moon make interior observations
continually: two sporous mushrooms surfacing
through peat like old bones, the peg
straddling the washing line, the flattened frog...

Who would have imagined the imagination could harden
into a list of strange symbols,
each entry with its own subtext of gloom?

When I was a girl the natural world terrified me.
I lay down on the grass and itched.

Now I thread my meals
with grass seed, let rain distil in my eyes.
I give myself to the sky the way a bat does
and still it pours clouds into my ears.

Neurosis: to feel in light rain
the onset of drowning.

The task: to recalibrate in a positive light.

Tongue to tongue the beech leaves shiver
in blue moonlight
and flashes of living things move through the overhead.

An owl and the wind call to me from the treetops as I bury
my head in the little white dots.

Cliff

Solicitous as any hurt person
      I lead my brother to the cliff edge,
palm of my hand against small of his back.

What fall from the cliff and live are
masked puffins, gulls, young gannets
      just learning to put out wings,
plunging and pulling up

above the sea's many tongues – these daily
unminuted miracles.
      Fabulous view or *Look at the view* I say,
although the sea's mouth is louder now
than the spoken word.

Rocks like full stops. Gulls shrink
to ash and sink into the horizon.
      And there is a tiny tanker: a boat
in a bath with removable men: one yellow,
one green, one red.

In the east, a church spire injects the sky
with neither sorrow nor pain but life everlasting.
      In the east, the sky lays out its promise of rain.

      At our ankles, in the blunt wind,
even the little pink campion heads are turning.

ANZHELINA POLONSKAYA, *translated by* *Andrew Wachtel*

'Everything moves toward the sea'

Everything moves toward the sea, to the
oily water where it slices gold,
to the dark, pyramidal cypresses.
To the gull, straining its sinews. And to the scent of the dry pines.
On the shiny car, to make sure the tresses fall
over the eyes and the monsieur ("maybe I could have that marzipan bun
for two francs twenty-five?"), will certainly mess everything up.
What's the translation of marzipan?
And how to ensure that the person exiting the room won't be betraying.
Note the imperfective verb, "to be betraying".
Just because the best is already past.
If only people knew how to ask the question "what for?"
And no one's to blame that life turned out like a bad dream, like a nightmare.

Unfinished Music

Out of all winters past
one rises in my throat.
A man passes into the mist,
into someone else's music.

You, O omnipotent sorrow,
earthly mask of repetition,
in your nights there'll be no sleep
until that last, that final one.

Beyond a door's scrape – a door's scrape,
and how many forgotten doors there are,
the snow will sing requiems, releasing
both the beloved and the unloved.

And what will the unheard drops
of icy blood say...
We lived, lived as we could
and died as best we knew.

Geological Fault of Human Beings

they hug each other while buried underground

Darkness 〜〜〜〜〜 ‹ ‹ ‹ ‹
Ennui is skeleton buried underground!
Accumulated below an atrocity of lead plates and bricks!
Gas ● ● ●
Gravity pressured by *concrete buildings*!
In the bottom of a lead pipe ——— innumerable moving faces!
The *candeia* flickers!
Fault of human beings!
Horses collapsed in the total darkness of mud!
Men roused from their last train slumber!
A craftsman coming out of the hospital with a bandaged arm!
High-voltage line!
Gas!
Respiration is gas!

Machines stopped ——— the factory is pale!
They're wires ——— eyes and lips and chests and legs!
Carnal desire ——— better off kissing a pig!
Who would substitute ● ●
there's no way a guy works while holding roses and lilies!
Love is not a **deck of cards** to predict the present!
Gas ● ● iron ● fatigue ——— contaminated brain!
——— A woman with giant eyeballs falling!
Kuku ● *kuku* ● *kuku* ●
 kii ● *kii* ● *kiki* ● *kiki* ● *ufuera!*
Laughter gets caught on electric lines under a cloudy sky ———
chaotic sparks!
 ✗ ✗ ✗ ✗ ✗
● ● ● ● ●
Pss pss pss leaking leaking leaking leaking leaking
morning ———after a "tired night" gone too far
white smoke drawing a line!
The sick ● **homicide** ● **the dead** ● *pistol*
Ennui being crushed across the ground!

from Death Sentence *by Hagiwara Kyojiro, translated by Sho Sugita.*

ANDRE BAGOO

from *The Scarlet Ibis*

Do they have a leader? Their

Do they have a leader? Their
 colonies are large, with as
  many as two thousand nests.
 Because of this, the scarlet ibis
contributes significantly to the
 energy wherever they live.
  In one wetland, the bird can be
 responsible for ten per cent of the
flow through the community.
 But they scatter after breeding
  season, wandering in smaller flocks,
 pairs, or as individuals, exploring
coast and rivers. Stragglers
 eventually return but do
  so under cover of night.
 They sleep perched together
in high trees. They sleep oddly:
 standing on one foot, bill and
  head gently resting on back.
 The males are more numerous.

The scarlet ibis lives only in America,
 on the tropical coasts of Venezuela,
  Trinidad, Guyana, Guiana,
Brazil, Suriname, Columbia.
The bird does not willingly go
 inland.   Storms have pushed it
  along the Caribbean islands, up
 the hurricane belt, through the Gulf
of Mexico, and Louisiana, and Texas,

and Carolina, Georgia, Florida.
 A single bird was spotted at
Corpus Christi, Texas, after
the storm of August 18, 1916.

Of this, a witness says:

> On one of the drifts that
> contained 31 dead cattle
> beside the bodies of 215
> birds of various kinds,
> there stood a solitary
> scarlet ibis. Like a
> garnet in the sands or
> a rosy promise of the
> morning sun, it stood,
> gracefully poised above the
> terrible ruin – an
> encouragement, an unfailing
> hope – not as the
> rainbow suggesting the
> possibility of another
> destructive force, but
> as an animated symbol
> that life is immortal.

Fresh or dried, the meat
 of the scarlet ibis has an
oily flavor. The birds
are shot while sitting on
 their eggs or standing beside
 their young, after which
they are salted or dried, and
transported in barrels to

the city. In Guyana in 1908,
 a bird sold for twenty-five
cents. Hunters, throughout
history, have gone out of their way
for the flesh of the scarlet ibis.
 They shoot the young birds,

travelling to the mouth of the
River Pomeroon, or the River Waini,
fearsome, mosquito-ridden spots.
 The hunters use devious traps.
They know the birds very well.
Narcissists, the scarlet ibis loves its
own color. So the hunters wave
 pieces of red cloth, as if in bloody
surrender, or they lay a red fish
with bright scales in an open space.

 Young birds can be tamed
 easily but never attain
the deep scarlet plumage
 of the free bird. Adults
 lose their brilliant color
in captivity. Persecution
and violence have had an
 effect upon the scarlet ibis,
 in making it watchful and
 retiring. Knowing without
knowing, truly unknown.
 Hunters and fishermen
 say the birds have grown
unapproachable over the years.
Notwithstanding its fears,
 the scarlet ibis has a deep

curiosity. It can watch
tourists for hours. It adopts
a pretext: pretending to forage
while surveying intruders.
This eager reconnaissance
does not always protect the bird.

Their eggs are green,

Their eggs are green,
newborns are black.
They turn grey, then white.
The young make a shrill cry
but after thirty-five days fly.
Both parents rear the young.
If one parent is killed,
others take up their duties.
After seventy-five days
the young are self-reliant.
Nothing like their parents,
they form separate flocks, travel
apart from the adults.
After three years,
THEY TURN COMPLETELY
SCARLET. Their heads are the last
limb to transform. Adults
measure twenty-three inches
in length, thirty-seven inches in
width. The bill is five inches long.
They weigh thirty-five pounds, so
they have to try harder when flying.
The tip of their bill is square.

Their legs are covered with large
scales. Their toes are webbed,
 they have claws. Legs are often
  mistaken for tails when in flight.
CORRECTION: Their
wingtips are deep blue, not black.
Of all the ibises, the scarlet ibis
 engages in the most hostile
communications: grunting, croaking,
honking, squealing, a gurgling gwe
 gwe, hissing, rattling – all have
  been reported.
They sometimes fly   in   single   file   forming

        a   line   –   an   interminable   line

ANITA PATI

Dodo Provocateur

Europeans hunted you mercilessly,

because you beakies wouldn't be doves or albatross.

Those whitish irises probably grotted and balled and seized,

black undertail coverts jutting at strumpet-starved sailors,

marooned on Mauritius, exotic, just not Bideford, Perth or Poole.

Why gobble pebbles big as nutmegs to temper your guts,

and prove fresh meat for rusky sailors, declaring you foul?

"Belly and breast pleasant enough in flavour," they said.

If only they'd waited a few decades later before they snuffed you

forever, for being cloven-footed, turkey! You know,

you and your bulging brethren could have been common as peacocks,

not stuffed through your hooks in old Copenhagen or folded in sketchbooks.

Mauritian Martha, who froze your fruity body in gin?

Now of the Marthas exists only bitty skin, you pigeons.

A.K. BLAKEMORE

dicks like jesus

three days of vestry weather
and the pinot hitting a stomach raw
to produce a lilac mood where simply everyone
is watching

we the shaved *en cas d'incendie* –
skimming death's-heads and dropping blows
through intercourse pearl-bordered
& replete with sense of whimsy –

imagination unseemly after four years
coiled on his pillow in pear-cut stones
asking

would you rather be shot or sued.
a white sphinx
with her academic specimen –

there are easier ways to make money but not tenure
so who here is the real victim?

escape high
into the rose-petal tartlet of a newborn day
with those boy sylphs in laundered kit
and frottage mirrored in the big moist eyes
of domestic cats. o dicks like jesus

so nice
so quiet
so kind to its mother

squirming like a moth on tile
beneath my purgative curve

waiting to be pinned and mounted
in the great silence when i – sated – pull away

mouse

mouse writes deep and lyrically vitreous poems about what it means to be alone...

mouse produces neurotic verse about discussing the fingers that went inside you... mouse sends acid missives from the world where you are very afraid to open the door...

mouse won't stop until she's pierced all your priests... mouse is a bright young bodily smell...

watch mouse
as she elegantly traverses the space between female academics and their velvet shrug jackets...

HUGO WILLIAMS

The Deal

If you feel like a change
you can swap your present condition
for a case of dizziness,
bed for breathlessness,
cramps for unconsciousness.
You can lower your blood pressure
in return for a sick headache,
bore yourself to death
watching wheels going round,
or die of blood poisoning.

When you've cut some sort of deal
with the laws of nature
you can totter out of there
in thrall to the velvet hour,
sensing around you
the promise of night-scented streets
and the recklessness of summer.
You wonder what you would give
in exchange for this.

Bucephalus

Dialysis two days running
produces an 'absence seizure',
a cerebral avalanche
of flints and sparks
which leaves me speechless.
I'm buried alive
in an abstract expression
of blizzards and ghosts,
blubbing, terrified, lost,
as I try but fail to exist.
The search for my face
in the snows of Mount Everest
is a hunt for the Yeti
in the world of ideas.

The sort of thing I don't know
when I sit up in bed
and look in the palm of my hand
is why things happen when we do them
and not before.
It's funny at first
when you raise your hand
to touch the alien fur
and all of a sudden
you don't know who you are.
It's supposed to come back to you
like the name of the Yeti,
but sometimes it doesn't
and they have to keep you in.

I've been trying to remember
the name of the beast
that has to forget itself
before it can begin.
I think it's the same
as Alexander's horse,
the one named after a bull
because of his swollen head.
I want it tattooed on my arm
in case I'm washed up somewhere
without my medical notes.
Thank God for the lever beside my bed
which raises and lowers
the steeple of Highgate Church.

A Marvel of the Age

I thought of The Old Operating Theatre
off Borough High Street,
"A Marvel of the Age" in 1821,
where students and doctors enjoyed
a state-of-the-art technology.
You enter via the spiral staircase
of the Southwark Cathedral Chapterhouse
and the antique smell of a herb loft,
looking down from the gods
on a wooden 'O', where the ghosts
of doctors and patients
rehearse their mortal pantomime.

The operating table takes centre stage
with its headrest and manacles,
its mop standing in a bucket,
its bloodstained aprons
hanging on a hook behind the door.
The vertiginous tiers of seating
have rails for the students to lean over,
drinking and shouting
to drown the screams of the principal,
as he struggles to free himself
from the terrible demands of his part.
He is giving the performance of a lifetime.

St Pancras Old Church and Hospital

I trace my footsteps
round this garden waiting room
where patients walk the line
between heaven and earth.

Great trees shed their prayers
on the silent company.
Stone books lie open forever
on forgotten endings.

I used to come here
every other day for years
with my books and sandwiches,
waiting to be reborn.

I would drag my feet
through the backsliding seasons
to a gate in the wall
with its notice of opening hours.

I passed my days
lying down with a machine,
till someone unknown to me died
and allowed me to go home.

Now here I am, a new man,
not quite myself perhaps,
yet able to ramble occasionally
in this twilit ante-room,
with only one foot in the grave.

RÓISÍN TIERNEY

Pity the Squid

as I dismember him
on the marble counter of our holiday let,
lift the tentacles away from his mantle,
peel off his mottled purplish skin,
remove his quill, as brittle as plastic,
rinse his cavity, wipe down his hood
(his hood, his hood, his moody hood!),
grope around to sever his beak.
I feel like a murderer, though I bought him dead,
snuggled in slush at the fish counter,
his queer squid eyes fixed on nothing.

Thrice-hearted, blue-blooded, jet-propeller
of the deeps – a little Lucifer! He changes colour
on a whim, up-ends himself to become
a frond of this or that, waving his arms about,
and so escapes his predators.
They are many, his enemies. I am one.
He has our scientists baffled, this
cleverest of the invertebrates,
noblest of the cephalopods,
king among molluscs!

He swims alone, mostly,
except for sex-orgies
that culminate
in one giant mass-ejaculation
on the ocean bed.

When he is frightened he has a trick –
with his sac he can eject
an exact squid-shaped copy of himself,

an inky pseudomorph,
which hangs, blurring, in the sea,
while he, the *real* he
swims away to safety.

All his art, his elegant deceptions,
his bioluminescent camouflage,
his arse-first, reckless self-propulsions,
his casting of smoke-screens,
his avatars,

have failed to save him from
this inglorious fate:
my chopping board, that pan, your plate,
arroz negro, chipirones, calamares.

JENNA CLAKE

Cloud Appreciation Society

Then came the day that we saw a cloud attached to a parachute,
heading down towards us...

We caught the cloud lovingly,
and asked if it wanted to stay with us...

It asked to keep the parachute on, and we let it...

And we took the cloud to bed with us, one by one,
not to sleep *with* it, but next to it...

We felt so wonderful with our arms wrapped around the cloud...

When it slept, it breathed like the sound inside a shell...

We were jealous when it slept
next to someone else...

We asked it to stay, and held it too tightly...

Before it left, it told us it would be back soon, but that it was a cloud,
and part of being a cloud was needing to move around...

We would have to open the window wide for it,
let it squeeze past us to get out...

We would watch it push itself into the sky
and parachute into the next house...

We felt a heavy rain in our stomachs...

ULRIKE ALMUT SANDIG, *translated by* Karen Leeder

Gold-Marie's dream

At the break of day, I lie awake and listen
to the aftermath of the night's noisy dreams

a high-speed chase through our house
that was sold to strangers long ago.

At the break of day, I listen to mother. She says
what I lacked in my head I made up for in my legs.
Mother was as speedy as an express train, airy as

a mobile network, invisible as data transfer
my, she was always everywhere, a finger in every pie.

In the cellar the lamp goes off and back on
in the kitchen all four gas rings are alight
in the bedroom there are piles of mattresses.

On the nightstand, a tea glass of ice-cream
is not what it seems, with an embedded jpeg

and a picture of a child hidden inside that
screams: hey, mother, where have you been?

Pitch-Marie's fever dream

Cock-a-doodle-doo, the dirty girl
is back here too! I am ugly, a lazy slut

and do I give a fuck? When the bread
called "take me out, take me out, or

I'll burn", I was busy contemplating
the shock front of particles in the blood-

orange sun storm, when the
apple tree called: "shake me

shake me, all of us apples are
ripe", I ate one. It was sweet

like All Souls, juicy like fresh
snow. The others I left there

for the grateful starlings. I lay
in the loathsome woman's sheets

scribbling notes and thought to myself: boy
will there be trouble

ENQUIRY

Essays on translation

. . .

Khairani Barokka
Translation of/as Absence, Sanctuary, Weapon

Translations are as complex as the concept of literatures at large – multiple, layered, shaped regionally and transnationally, never neutral, always deeply nuanced, inflected with cultural biases and the baggage of cultural workers. Ever employed, in this year as always, to advance political mindsets, to continue or disrupt regimes of language. The blanket application of false binaries to encompass one work, such as 'transparency' versus 'opacity', or 'accessible' language versus 'inaccessible' language, is shown to be reductive and broken open in two examples here that demonstrate translation as always bodily. In both Cok Sawitri's performance of bravado and deliberate withholding of translation, as well as in the conceptual framework for my book *Indigenous Species*, creative choices reveal what assumptions of translation we can work to dismantle: how the notions of absence, sanctuary, and weapon are employed. In particular, these frameworks reveal how deeply, indelibly translations are tied to perpetuating or unpacking ableist, colonialist notions of the 'good' bodymind.

I. Cok and the Night Ambush

Several years ago, at the Ubud Writers and Readers Festival opening ceremony, Balinese poet, theatre artist, and activist Cok Sawitri gave a bravura performance – open-air, under the stars, surrounded by traditional local architecture and a plenitude of foreign tourists and writers. Senior performer Cok did not circle that space as much as prowl it, hilariously monologuing in Indonesian and Balinese on tourism's impacts on her home province, local homestay owners putting their bodily detritus in banana pancakes, the 'paradise island' myth beaming in tourists' imaginations. She was ferociously shattering myths of locals as ready to appease, to heal, and to cater to foreigners' whims, of the island, struggling under the weight of overdevelopment and environmental destruction, as existing purely for incomers. Pulsing throughout her piece was the blatant discrepancy between what outsiders expect of Bali, and the performative acts of compliance, as well as acts of resistance, that Balinese people enact in the face of them.

'The Night Ambush' is not the title of the piece, but my own personal naming of this performance, how I remember it. The genius guile here: Cok performed the piece in two local languages, in front of swathes of foreigners who understood neither. She was teasing them at a high-profile literary event in Southeast Asia, without them being the wiser – to them, she was a woman attired in elaborate Balinese clothing, running around vocalising what was probably a sacred traditional welcome. When all of us, non-Balinese and Balinese Indonesians, as well as foreigners, clapped loudly for her together, we were clapping *for entirely different reasons.* Those of us who understood Cok's monologue, untranslated that night, were complicit in her conceit, and it made us proud. Those who did not understand her words and clapped were, with their applause, extending the piece's affect, confirming how successful it was, a double-edged sword.

This remains one of my dearest memories of performance of any kind. It was one I will always feel privileged to have been privy to, particularly for being one of those in attendance who was Indonesian-fluent but not Balinese-fluent, both outsider and insider. I am Indonesian but not Balinese, though I have Balinese cousins and friends who live on the island, and have often visited. By virtue of Indonesian-fluency, I understood the code-switching and richly layered sociopolitical critique at play, and the stratification of Cok's intended audience. Yes, it was for Indonesians and

Indonesian-speakers, but only to a certain extent. Most of all, it was for Balinese people, those local to Ubud in particular. What could easily have been yet another act of cultural production primarily for outsider consumption became one of generative and covert, yet wildly open, refusal. To my knowledge, the script has never been published nor translated into English, lending further power to Cok's cunning move through her work's ephemerality.

Years later, reminiscing, the question arises: what if there had been sign-language interpreters at Cok Sawitri's aforementioned performance? The notion of inclusivity here becomes inclusivity for whom, and to what ends? Which sign languages would have been used – or would there only have been one? If so, which one: Australian Sign Language (Auslan), reflecting the origins of most festival attendants, thereby including only D/deaf Australians in on the grand scheme? BISINDO, the term for Indonesian Sign Language? It might seem most implausible that there would be any interpretation in Kata Kolok, a sign language indigenous to only one village in Bali, which has a disproportionate number of D/deaf residents and has proudly developed a language of its own. Choices of sign languages, as for any other languages, are political.

What if there had been audio description at the performance? Audio description too is never 'objective'; the description itself is a scripted performance, and when conceptualised as its own artwork has ignited exciting possibilities. Would there have been a split between an audio description of it in English, in Balinese, and in Indonesian?

The absence of translation in Cok's performance was a beautiful sanctuary for her defiance and our basking in it, yet as every single artwork is, it is partial sanctuary. The absence of translation for D/deaf Indonesians made it partial sanctuary of a very different kind than the absence of translation in Auslan, and if the latter had been chosen over the former (if there could only be one choice of sign language), I believe this decision would have gone against Cok's principles.

A disability justice framework for translation requires an understanding of nuance, a comprehension that there are gradations of absence, of sanctuary, and of translation as weapon. Having sign language translation in BISINDO and Kata Kolok, but not in Auslan, for instance, would have been weaponry in keeping with Cok's creation of sanctuary, for respite from having to exist in one's own land as fodder for others' fantasies. Yet would the very announcement of these translations have been a 'tell' that gave away the artist's plan?

Translation that may be a shared sanctuary, a bridging to some, is an absence of this connectivity for others, and not always in ways we've internalised as intuitive. There is nothing that has been translated into every language ever known and used, especially as more and more languages face extinction at an alarming rate. The subject of which languages and poetries are chosen for translation, and how they are translated, is always infused with biases.

Understanding gradations of absence, of sanctuary, and of translation as weapon also requires an innate humility of all that we as individuals do not know, and have yet to learn, in order to translate with requisite awareness: that feminisms are as plural as literatures, and that western or white feminisms are not the same as Indonesian feminisms, with different regional histories and emphases – this matters for an analysis of Cok's performance. For instance, I come from a matrilineal culture, Minangkabau, that predates use of the word "feminism" by centuries, yet I now proudly call these West Sumatran roots feminist.

Further, ''65–'66' does not mean the same thing to Indonesian feminists as it does to those from elsewhere – these are the years of state-sanctioned mass murder, with victims possibly in the millions, targeting minorities and those accused of being leftists, including many feminist organisers, and was at heart a legacy of the Cold War. Yet I have read text after text after text that presumes to subsume all of the world's women into a version of 'the sixties' that is Eurocentric or US-centric, even as the politics of those retellings are indelibly tied to what Indonesian feminists endured. I'm not sure Cok would entrust a translation of her poetic ambush that night in Bali years ago to someone who did not know these histories, to someone unaware that Bali contains mass graves as much as it does tourist resorts.

By the same token – just as a word such as "feminism" is loaded with knowings and unknowings and the deliberate ways politics and economics shape what we know and are not meant to know – there is an innumerable variety of kinds of bodyminds on the planet, contributing to linguistic diversity that remains unacknowledged. Even those of us who identify as disabled (with many, but not all, taking the social model approach whereby the term implies the opposite of 'enabled', not 'unable'), who've worked in disability studies and research, are liable to be completely unaware of various kinds of languages used, whether sign languages, Brailles, the languages of autistic people and communities, and on and on. These languages are also regionally and historically shaped. These languages are also less likely to be treated as languages worthy of being translated into and from, as literatures and poetries to be archived, disseminated, studied in schools and universities, celebrated in all the ways some languages belonging to more normative bodies are.

The offshoot of these inequities is that bodies to whom those languages belong continue to be disenfranchised, excluded, and endangered. I am thinking here particularly of artist Amanda Baggs's video 'In My Language' (available on YouTube), which uses the word 'translation' quite prominently to convey the discrepancy between how people perceive her communication as an autistic person, and what she is actually conveying:

> We are even viewed as non-communicative if we don't speak the standard language but other people are not considered non-communicative if they are so oblivious to our own languages as to believe they don't exist. [...] And in a world in which those determine whether you have any rights there are people being tortured, people dying because they are considered non-persons because their kind of thought is so unusual as to not be considered thought at all.

Biases regarding the 'good' bodymind shape language, and language – as we know – shapes the felt world, and moulds what universe our selves as bodyminds live through. These biases have historically been shaped, in Indonesia, by colonial regimes for hundreds of years, including Dutch and English. In his book *Disability in Java: Contesting Conceptions of Disability in Javanese Society after the Suharto Regime* (2013), Slamet Thohari explains how colonial and missionary medicine created a preponderance of the medical model of disability on Indonesia's most populous island, in which all non-normative bodies are seen as impaired and in need of cure, regardless of whether or not the people involved perceive themselves as such.

In other words, the likelihood that any poetic performance in Indonesia will be translated into BISINDO or another sign language, be audio-described, or be a 'relaxed' performance inclusive of disabled bodyminds, for instance, has been decimated by deliberate choices to regard certain bodies as less-than- or non-human. Thus we lose chances to disseminate poetry. Thus we lose chances to honour poets in non-abled languages, and to create more poets in those languages. Thus we lose chances for people to learn about their poetic heritages of languages outside those perceived as normative.

II. Indigenous Species

Thinking of translation as a cleaving, a refracting, I think of how the word 'refracting' calls to mind for me (coded as a seeing person despite severe short-sightedness, only because glasses and contacts are not as stigmatised as other assistive devices) a ray of light's direction being manipulated, and how this word, as a visual image, is tied to its ocularcentricity. When I first began to delve into the world of arts research from disability justice frameworks, in 2011, I became aware of how cultural consumption is skewed towards those of us both hearing and seeing. As though blind and sight-impaired artists don't also create and come from cultures of their own, as though D/deaf cultures aren't linguistically rich.

Sharing screenshots of poems on social media without captioning them – either in the body of the text or through the new option to caption images on Twitter, for instance – is an act of exclusion from poetry for blind and sight-impaired readers, as much as an act of inclusion into poetry for seeing people. Ocularcentricity is societally shaped, as is audiocentricity, and verticalcentricity (I say as I currently write these words in a horizontal position, assumed most hours of most days so I will be able to be vertical for more often when I choose to be; full disclosure).

Part of my project with my book *Indigenous Species*, informed by the work blind and sight-impaired artist-activists have long been doing, is a translation of absence: the word Braille in 'flat Braille' is on every left-hand page, to emphasise to sighted readers that we are, in fact, sighted readers. Originally conceived as a sight-impaired accessible art book, which grew out of a poem first written and performed for the Emerging Writers Festival in Melbourne, Australia in 2013, I stipulated to the publisher that there would be a "sighted version" that proclaimed itself as such. I tried to create enough contrast on the illustrated pages, so that as many colour-blind readers as possible would be able to see the artwork. In addition, two kinds of accessible e-books were created of the book for purchase.

The hope is that in addition to ensuring more accessibility for non-seeing demographics, an awareness is created in multiple ways for sighted readers: of the absence of access in publishing, made more prominent when one understands a book as object, but also the absence of access to blind and sight-impaired cultures for us sighted people. "Plain sight" is never just that. Sightedness and gearing arts resources towards sightedness – and hearingness, neurotypicalness, etc. – is political, as being a cis-gender woman is political, as living and breathing in the United Kingdom is political, as visa statuses are political, as the sources of our breakfasts are political, as our choice of poetry consumption and production and engagement beyond and within capitalist models is political.

It is difficult to categorise such translation of absence as "opaque" or "transparent", considering both terms are so clearly only of seeing cultures and thus limited, but also because one could ask what is being made transparent, and how. If I say I am making absence of language to blind readers on a flat page "transparent" for sighted readers, was it not the case that those of us who are sighted readers already knew that flat pages of a paperback book – without audiobooks, accessible e-book versions and Braille – are inaccessible to blind and sight-impaired readers? What socialisation has made this exclusion seem natural?

As with every translation or artistic project, *Indigenous Species* as intended weapon, absence, and sanctuary has limits. Not all blind and sight-impaired people use or read Braille, for one, so there is that generalisation. However, it feels like a small gesture in response to sighted privilege, as a sighted creator who has learned from the work of many blind and sight-impaired creators, apart from the story itself as gesture, that of an abducted girl in a river boat trying to escape, conveying her thought process with power, fiercely aware of the environmental destruction around her, and its social consequences. It feels like only one of many, many possibilities to respond to the limiting of respect and care for bodyminds deemed to be aberrant, unimportant, used as imagery in abled writers' poetry yet still excluded as poets and poetry lovers.

I think of Cok's calling out of the forces pushing us to perform for a western gaze, of all the ways culture pushes us to perform for an abled gaze, how these norms of bodily functioning have contributed to current policies in Indonesia, in the UK, and elsewhere, elevation of certain bodies and desires and ways of connecting with literature over others. I think of how translation in poetry can always be, in myriad ways, absence, sanctuary, and weapon.

Khairani Barokka, Indigenous Species, *Tilted Axis, £15/£7.99, ISBN 9781911284048 (print) / 9781911284055 (Braille)*

Sophie Collins
Erasing the signs of labour under the signs of happiness: 'joy' and 'fidelity' as bromides in literary translation

A couple of years ago I attended an inaugural address by a professor of translation who had been newly appointed to a university near where I live. I wasn't a member of the university community, in any sense (neither a student nor a member of staff there), but had long been an admirer of the professor and, having read that the address would pertain specifically to the translation of poetry, decided to go along. On the day of the lecture I boarded a train and made my way to the university from the station at the other end. Once on campus, I navigated my way through various grey corridors and laminated stairwells until I reached the small lecture room. I sat down and took out my notebook, placing it on the narrow desk in front of me.

I wrote down very little in the following forty-five minutes; I was grossly disappointed by the lecture. The professor's opening gambit was this: having worked in translation for decades, and written many a critical text (in both senses of the phrase), they had become exhausted by discussions of literary translation that centred on its "negative" aspects, whatever these may be (there was no distinction made here between different types of negativity – a compelling term which itself remained undefined – and no attention to questions of intent). From now on, the professor had said, they would be focusing uniquely on the *joy of translation*, a mission statement that was duly accompanied by a number of other platitudes...

My own experience of literary translation throughout the past five years (my experience with translation in a broader sense goes back to childhood) has so far generated an appetite for the precise opposite. This disparity of feeling – of desire – derives in part, I think, from the distinct nature of academic discussions of literary translation and those put forward by poets and literary critics. An articulation of the differences between these two would warrant its own essay (or at least more words than I have to spend on contrasting them here), but, based on my perspective – as someone who has worked primarily as a poet – and that of the above professor, it suffices to say that where academic discussions of literary translation were significantly influenced by the proliferation of postcolonial and feminist texts in the late twentieth century,[1] poets and literary critics often appear to never have heard of the arguments put forward by Gayatri Spivak, Kwame Anthony Appiah, Tejaswini Niranjana, Homi K. Bhabha, Julia Kristeva, Hélène Cixous, etc., etc. – or, if indeed they have, are evidently unable to figure these in terms of translation, which is connected to its continuing perception as a neutral, transparent process (poets' versions, which are often based on a so-called 'literal' or 'bridge' translation, are thought to be something quite different).

For me, with my involvement in poetry outdating that of my engagement with literary translation, the emphasis that is consistently placed, in the latter context, on the so-called *joy of translation* (italicised here to labour my view of the phrase as a misnomer) is what is dispiriting. My translating literature – poetry and prose – from the Dutch evokes feelings of uncertainty and self-consciousness, and – perhaps more frequently than might be imagined – breakdown and frustration. Sometimes I feel fulfilled and excited by the interaction; sometimes it exacerbates my persisting imposter syndrome: the uneasy sense that, having now lived in the UK continuously for a decade, I no longer have a stake or claim in the language and culture that fostered me for fourteen years during the most influential stage of life, from childhood into young adulthood. At other moments, there can of course be an enjoyable sense of gratification when my capabilities of expression in the English and comprehension of the Dutch source text allow me to connect with, and to further the scope of, the poem or novel and its author. Affect proliferates in the translation process, and enjoyment or pleasure might manifest at some point during, or on either side of, it, but the phrase the *joy of translation* shares a certain vapidity with the language of advertising that is, I believe, symptomatic of its actual and insidious function.

In *The Promise of Happiness* (2010), Sara Ahmed writes of the "critique of happiness as an affirmative gesture", a statement which might, on first reading, appear somewhat paradoxical. But what Ahmed is in fact proposing is that such a critique represents possibility because that which we have come to accept or recognise as 'happiness' is merely a kind of cultural 'promise' tendered "for having the right associations". "In wishing for

---

1. *This is arguable: in his preface to the new edition of* The Translator's Invisibility *(2008), Lawrence Venuti relates how many university translation departments and programmes continue to treat translation as a linguistics, rather than a humanities discipline.*

happiness," writes Ahmed, "we wish to be associated with happiness, which means to be associated with its associations." Such associations, suggests Ahmed, are represented by the dominant values of a given society, and so the individual's search for happiness is often simply the gradual acquiescence to dominant mores. A critique of 'happiness' is thus a critique of happiness as a social construct, one that frequently acts to preclude statements that are perceived as negative, despite the fact that such statements can represent vital and potentially ground-breaking critique. "Revolutionary forms of political consciousness," states Ahmed, "involve heightening our awareness of just how much there is to be unhappy about. Given that the desire for happiness can cover signs of its negation, a revolutionary politics has to work hard to stay proximate to unhappiness."

I see 'joy' in much the same way, as a word that no longer describes an internal, affective experience, but that has come to signify something more like obedience to a collective cause. In a recent interview published on the Asian American Writers Workshop website, poet and translator Don Mee Choi was asked what "the greatest joy" of translating Korean to English is. From her response:

> I am terrified of English. And because I have lived outside of South Korea for a long time, I've become a foreigner to Korean as well. In other words, I am a failure of language in general. So joy does not come to mind easily when I think about translating from Korean to English. I also associate joy with 'Joy of this and that' I saw and heard everywhere when I first came to this country [the US], including green-coloured JOY detergent. It was the first dish soap I used after my arrival. I wondered, even in my state of devastation having just separated from my family, why this nation was so obsessed with joy when it causes so much misery all over the world.

Here Choi consolidates an understanding of 'joy' as a conformist trope – in this instance, a verbal deposit of the imperial mindset, so ubiquitous in Anglophone countries as to be used to sell washing-up liquid. Ahmed also links her formulation of 'happiness' to the domestic realm, referencing Betty Friedan's debunking of the myth of "the happy American housewife" in *The Feminine Mystique* (1963):

What lies behind this image bursts through, like a boil, exposing an infection underneath her beaming smile. Friedan proceeds by exposing the limits of this public fantasy of happiness. The happy housewife is a fantasy figure that erases the signs of labor under the sign of happiness. The claim that women are happy and that this happiness is behind the work they do functions to justify gendered forms of labor, not as a product of nature, law or duty, but as an expression of a collective wish and desire. How better to justify an unequal distribution of labor than to say that such labor makes people happy? How better to secure consent to unpaid or poorly paid labor than to describe such consent as the origin of good feeling?

Erasing the signs of labour under the sign of happiness: this perfect phrase of Ahmed's encapsulates what I'm trying to express here, that *the joy of translation* is troubling not because I have an issue with its fundamental proposition, i.e., that translation is enjoyable, but that the application of the phrase reduces its affect to a sign, one that is in some way intended to justify the lack of professional and artistic recognition, and the inequitable pay that translators still receive.

The gendered language of translation and its effects on perceptions of the translation practice have been documented and analysed. In her brilliant *Gender in Translation: Culture, Identity and the Politics of Transmission* (1996), Sherry Simon draws lines between women and translators as having historically represented "the weaker figures in their respective hierarchies", linking such perceptions to power dynamics and biological reproduction:

> translators are handmaidens to authors, women inferior to men. [...] Whether affirmed or denounced, the femininity of translation is a persistent historical trope. 'Woman' and 'translator' have been relegated to the same position of discursive inferiority. The hierarchical authority of the original over the reproduction is linked with imagery of masculine and feminine; the original is considered the strong generative male, the translation the weaker and derivative female. We are not surprised to learn that the language used to describe translating dips liberally into the vocabulary of sexism, drawing on images of dominance and inferiority, fidelity and libertinage.

In 'Gender and the Metaphorics of Translation' (1988), Lori Chamberlain adds that such metaphors (which include the notorious adage "Les belles infidèles") are consolidated by the dominance of capitalist beliefs, given that translations have, like "conventional representations of women", been determined by "a cultural ambivalence about the possibility of a woman artist and about the status of a woman's 'work'". Referencing the work of feminist art critics, including Linda Nochlin, Chamberlain writes that gendered cultural models that enable claims such as the infamous "there are no great women artists" differentiate between "productive" and "reproductive" work, presenting "originality or creativity in terms of paternity and authority" and "relegating the figure of the female to a variety of secondary roles". The act of translating, she continues, is frequently discussed in the "secondary terms" attributed women's creative acts, and is thus clearly "seen as qualitatively different from the original act of composing [...] from the original act of writing".

It's clear, then, that in order to challenge a deeply entrenched perception of translators and translations as culturally inferior, we must alter the language and metaphors used to articulate and envision the translation process. 'Joy' is not only a means through which to keep translation at the bottom of the creative hierarchy identified by Simon and Chamberlain, but one that mystifies the translation process by insisting on its positive aspects and limiting discussion of its complex or 'negative' ones.

'Fidelity' is another such mystifying term. As Chamberlain suggests, 'fidelity', which recalls marriage, implies the presence of a (masculine-coded) primary power whose laws the translation, and so too the translator, must recognise and adhere to. The source of legislation, however, is in fact rarely specified in literary contexts, or, I believe, conceived of at all. Looked at closely, reviews or critiques of translations that apply the terms 'fidelity' or 'faithfulness' do not tend to compare the translation directly to the source text (the poem being translated), but rather to a particular reading or understanding of that source text. This means that a translation can be judged 'wrong' or 'incorrect' by a critic or reviewer when it doesn't match their own linguistic or thematic interpretation of the source poem, which is often presented as, and very much thought by the critic or reviewer to be, universal or definitive.

Maintaining the analogy of interlingual translation as a relationship between source text author and translator, I tentatively offer 'intimacy' – which I use in the Platonic sense of 'close familiarity or friendship', rather than euphemistically – as a term that can establish the basis for an alternative conceptualisation of translations and the translation process. This coinage began with the observation that, while 'fidelity' implies the presence of a primary source of power, 'intimacy' indicates a mutual, consensual and willing exchange between two or more subjects, without referencing (an) authority at all.

Intimacy is a notoriously nebulous concept. What we can say, however, with some degree of confidence, is that to build intimacy with another person is to become 'close' to them. In human relationships, this becoming 'close' involves a physical and intellectual proximity – or perhaps, in the digital age, a purely cerebral closeness that is the product of frequent exchanges, by email, text and/or social media messaging. This exchange of thoughts and information establishes the conditions for what we implicitly understand as the root of intimacy, i.e., an understanding of the other's background and history, and so too of their personal motivations and desires.

In terms of approaches to translation, then, 'intimacy' surely describes work that exhibits such closeness, meaning that an 'intimate translation' might be one that exhibits a heightened contextualisation of its source text for the reader. Choi, as a translator with (to put it lightly) a stated distaste for conventional models within poetry translation and who has declared, frequently and directly, a particular closeness to one of her source text authors, Kim Hyesoon, might already be enacting the idea of 'intimacy' in translation. In fact, given my deep admiration for her approach, I think it's quite possible that I've unconsciously tailored my notion of 'intimacy' to her innovative and necessarily political translations.

Choi's work with Kim Hyesoon's poetry has been made available to readers not only through the volumes of translations published in the US and UK, but in the many texts written by Choi about her translation process. Through such texts, Choi has established what we might term a 'radical commentary', a continuous dialogue on her work with Kim that transcends the conventional boundaries of the translator's preface or afterword, both physically and in terms of its content. The most concentrated example of Choi's radical commentary can be found in *Freely Frayed, ㄱ=q, & Race=Nation* (2014), a limited edition pamphlet published by Wave Books, which brings together the texts of three talks given by Choi at various writing and translation conferences. In one of the texts, Choi writes that "contextualising the work may be the most important part of [her] translation process", whereas discussion of "why this word and not that word" is something she experiences as "suffocating". Taking up, with theatrical realism, the position of the "lowly" translator, she indicates that the perception of translators as 'faithful' intermediaries is insufficient when it comes to describing the creative and emotional labour of her process:

> See You Later Translator. No, I'm not an agitator. It turns out that I'm a mere imitator, the lowly kind, which is none other than a translator a mimicker of mimetic words in particular. Doubled consonants or certain parts of speech that are repeated on certain occasions, which can be said to be nobody's business, but they are since everything in English is everybody's business. *Farfar swiftswift zealzeal stuffstuff waddlewaddling stickysticky cacklecackled draindrained flowflow yellyell swishswish.* I've just been instructed to get rid of them by an evaluator: Why double up? No, I'm not a collaborator. I'm actually very frail, frailer than a Thumbelina in the world of everybody's business. In my world of nobody's business I twirl about frantically frequently farfar to the point of failure feigning englishenglish.

In another contextualising text, 'Translation–Darkness–Migration', published on the Poetry Foundation website, Choi writes directly of the sense of dislocation experienced as a result of her family's leaving South Korea for Hong Kong during the former's military dictatorship following the May 16 coup, in which Park Chung Hee and the Military Revolutionary Committee (as backed by US military forces) regained control of the state from North Korea. Utilising the commentary space to prioritise the political interpretation of her source text and translation process is thus an approach that is both truer to Choi's experience of engagement with the source text and the way in which she translates.

A second key quality that I believe to be a feature of 'intimate translations' relates to the translator's exhibited interlingual play. Cultural theorist Lauren Berlant has written in the introduction to her edited volume *Intimacy* (2000) that "[to] intimate is to communicate with the sparest of signs and gestures, and [that] at its root intimacy has the quality of eloquence and brevity". In the same anthology, poet Maureen McLane claims that, conversely, "one of the most remarkable and telling features of [intimacy as an affective state] is its profoundly romantic interest in linguistic profusion and the disjunctions between and within bodies and languages". For me, both statements contain elements of emotional truth, and I think it might rather be the case that the fluctuations in tone represented by the ability of individuals to comfortably inhabit both states around one another is what best characterises the condition of intimacy.

When I first encountered Choi's translations of Kim in the Bloodaxe book *I'm OK, I'm Pig!* (2014), which brings together the work of three distinct US publications, it seemed to me that there was a very particular sound to Choi's translations of Kim, one that was both present in the first translated poem in the collection (first published by Action Books, in the US, in 2008), and that also appeared to have escalated over time, its hallmarks more overt in the book's final texts (from 2011). The most immediate idiosyncratic sonic feature is the anaphora and other forms of repetition that pervade the book. The insistent and effusive tone this establishes in the mind and mouth of the reader is what caused me to first link Choi's translations to concepts of intimacy and friendship.

My emails to my best friend are filled with in-jokes, capitalised and repeated words (for effect or emphasis), neologisms and an approximation – often via added vowels – of the kind of croaky 'vocal fry' and twangy 'high rising terminal' that is negatively associated with young women's speech. In *I'm OK, I'm Pig!* these quirks are similarly borne out in the anaphora, exclamation marks, onomatopoeic laughter and Choi's neologistic repetitions: "kisskiss", "coldcold", "plopplop", "gulpgulp". As above, such idiosyncrasies have frequently been subject to scrutiny by editors and proofreaders who understand them as errors on Choi's part. Even if we don't view them in this way, however, it would be easy to attribute the characteristics of Choi's translations entirely to Kim's source texts – most reviewers do, given Kim's distinct poetics. In her preface to *I'm OK, I'm Pig!*, Kim talks (in a translation also rendered by Choi) about her desire to develop a voice in Korean that explores "the possibilities of the sensory", that believes in its "own feminine individuation, its secrets", its own capacity to be "combative, visceral, subversive, inventive and ontologically feminine". Choi has also discussed her translation process in terms of the disparity between Korean and English – a political-linguistic gap that means that any translation from the Korean must necessarily be one of a more "intralingual" paraphrasing or "rewording", in Roman Jakobson's terms. But Choi's translations are not merely the result of the coalescence of these factors, something that can be easily recognised by reading her texts against those of Kim's other English-language translators (see, for example, Vanessa Falco and Kim Sunghyun's collaborative translations on the *World Literature Today* website).

As a proposed ideal for translations, 'intimacy' brings with it its own questions, problematics and risks. Ultimately, however, my application of the term is intended to shift the translation relationship from a place of universality, heteronormacy, authority and centralised power, towards a particularised space whose aesthetics are determined by the two or more people involved, in this way amplifying and promoting creativity and deviant aesthetics in translations between national languages.

During the writing of this text, having restated the links between the identity of 'translator' and that of 'woman' or 'female', what has struck me is the way in which the feelings of alienation, shame and irritation I experience in the face of *the joy of translation* have become perhaps less puzzling as I liken them to those that rise up in me when a man on the other side of the street commands me to "Cheer up!" or "Smile!"

In consistently arguing for the political interpretation of translations and of the process of translating, I know I will be conceived by many in terms of Ahmed's "killjoy figure". An increasingly popular line of discourse asserts that expressing 'negative' opinions doesn't solve or add anything, whereas love (which is equated with 'understanding' or 'empathy') can. To reject what is perceived as 'hate' or critique (the two are increasingly conflated) and express only so-called positive views is presented as the authentically revolutionary approach. This is something with which I passionately disagree. The critique of translation culture is, to my mind, a powerful expression of hope because it affirms the possibility of change. Without such hope many of the texts I have cited throughout this short essay would have ceded to despondency or apathy long before completion.

In the abovementioned interview, Choi says that her politically charged translation work is what gives her "much joy" – that's the affective state, and not the oppressive, mystifying, placating sign.

Carole Satyamurti
Retelling the Mahabharata

> "[...] all translation is only a somewhat provisional way of coming
> to terms with the foreignness of languages"
> – Walter Benjamin

The relationship between an original poem and its translated version encompasses a wide spectrum of possible strategies. At one end, the original serves as a springboard from which a new poem is created, where the relation of the new poem to the original may be barely discernible. At the other end, the translation is as close as possible to a literal equivalent of the original.

At some point, the translator-poet will have in mind the reader/listener receiving the new poem, and the effect s/he wants that poem to have. If s/he can assume familiarity with the original, whether in the original language or in other versions, there is more scope for play, in what we might call the translational space. So, for instance, Ted Hughes in *Tales from Ovid* could assume that at least some of his readers would be familiar with Ovid's poem in some form.

There are also ethical considerations. What does the poet owe to the original poem and its author? Can s/he cannibalise it or reshape it at will, or is there some obligation to respect the choices of the original poet, if the work is to be called a representation – re-presentation – of the pre-existing poem? Should s/he make clear to the reader, in a foreword perhaps, the way s/he has approached the work? If it is called a translation – and, of course, the term 'translation' itself is a contested one – should that always denote adherence, as far as possible, to the literal meanings of the original? How can differences in culture be taken into account, and respect given to the poem's culture of origin? These issues, among others, were very much on my mind as I began work on an English retelling of the *Mahabharata*.

The *Mahabharata* is one of the two great epic poems of India, the other being the *Ramayana*. At roughly three million words, it is probably the longest poem in the world, composed about two thousand years ago. As in other examples of the epic genre, its main theme is conflict – in this case, the struggle between two sets of royal cousins for possession of the kingdom of the Bharatas. This central story is the structure that holds together the vast narrative edifice and, around it, a huge cast of characters, an enormous array of stories and episodes, parables and instructive dialogues, is built. The entire poem takes the form of one person speaking to another, starting with the original narrator, a brahmin reciting the story to a royal descendant of the protagonists. As one actor speaks to another the epic unfolds, in some ways, like a nest of Chinese boxes.

Perhaps this makes the *Mahabharata* sound like an unwieldy mess, and that is largely how it was seen by Macaulay, Kipling and other servants of the British Raj who took the *Iliad* as their model of what an epic poem should be like. Even today, the *Mahabharata* is sometimes referred to in the West (when it is mentioned at all) as if it were merely a collection of stories or folk-tales, rather than a coherent work of art of enormous grandeur.

In embarking on my version of the *Mahabharata*, I was aware that, with very few exceptions, the prospective reader would be unfamiliar with the full original text. In its country of origin, certain stories from the epic, as well as the outline of the plot, are well known (especially among Hindus), and are reproduced on screen, in graphic image, children's stories and so on, and in the many regional languages. The *Bhagavad Gita*, which forms the heart of the epic, is widely revered as a free-standing sacred text which, in its narrative context, vividly presents the timeless difficulty of reconciling one's duty with responsibility for the consequences of one's actions.

But I would guess that few people have read the entire work, still fewer in the original Sanskrit. And in what may broadly be called the English-speaking West, it is probably true to say that most people have barely heard of it, even people educated in the humanities. I have sometimes suspected a deep ethnocentrism, even where I least expected it – an unexamined assumption that an ancient Indian epic is unlikely to have anything relevant to say to today's Western readers. My aim has been to convince them otherwise. I wanted to expand their horizon. I felt a responsibility to the original text – to make it live, in a form that the unfamiliar – even wary – reader in the West would relate to.

The question of 'ownership' of the text has also presented itself in some quarters. How can I, as an English person, inheritor of involvement in colonial oppression, and without a knowledge of Sanskrit, justify embarking on an English version of India's great epic? In response, I would simply say that the *Mahabharata* is no more the 'property' of Indians than the *Iliad* is the property of the Greeks. It is a great pillar of world literature and it is

– as it says of itself – intended for everyone, no matter what their birth.

Over the years, because of my interest in India, I had read a number of versions of it, all prose, and all abridgements, aimed at the general reader. But I knew that the original was a Sanskrit poem and, when I explored further, I increasingly felt that these relatively short prose versions did not do full justice to the scope and power of the original, or to its musical qualities when recited or chanted. At that time (about twelve years ago), there was only one complete translation of the epic available in English. It was a prose version, by K.M. Ganguli, dating from the late nineteenth century, and running to around 5,000 closely printed pages. The prose style is old-fashioned, but it conveys the depth and richness of the epic in a way that seemed to me to be missing in the more recent versions. In constructing my retelling, inevitably an abridgement, I drew on Ganguli's translation, as well as other, more recent, scholarly translations of parts of the epic. By avoiding other people's abridgements, I felt I could get as close as was possible to the original source. I also listened to recitations of the original Sanskrit shlokas (verses), not understanding the language, and not in order to reproduce the cadences, which would have been impossible, but to experience something of the musicality the ancient Indian audience would have heard, and then to aim for an English equivalent.

Why render the epic in verse, rather than in prose? The shloka was a strict verse form used in ancient India for a wide range of subject matter, including practical manuals, and for that reason it has been argued that it was the equivalent of prose today. But the shloka is patterned language, and is therefore, in my view, poetry – a view supported by the sound of the Sanskrit text when spoken aloud. I therefore decided to render it in poetic form, in flexible blank verse, with nine to eleven syllables to the line. Blank verse, arguably, occupies a similar place in the English literary tradition to the role played by the shloka in ancient Sanskrit. The diction of the original is relatively plain (the *Ramayana* is more 'poetic'), and I chose to render the epic in language that does not draw attention to itself, but is intended, like the original, to be read aloud.

Abridgement, of course, involved choices – judgements about which sections it was essential to include, in how much detail, and which could be left out. There are two sections, in particular, that most versions for the general reader treat much more cursorily than the original. One of these is the great war at Kurukshetra, the climax of the rivalry between the two sets of cousins. The other is the extensive teaching given to the newly victorious king by the dying patriarch – instruction about how a king should rule which bears some comparison with the strictures of Machiavelli. In Ganguli's translation, these sections occupy many hundreds of pages. In both cases, I felt that they deserved more space than they have usually been given. They are full of action; full of food for thought.

The *Mahabharata* hardly ever directly describes the inner worlds of the protagonists. Everything is conveyed through speech, and through action. Occasionally, in my version, I have not followed this example, where it is clear from the text what a character is feeling. My method was to read Ganguli, and other scholarly translations, section by section, and then to put them aside, and give myself time to digest what I had read, intellectually, emotionally and aesthetically. Out of this process would come a decision about what to include, to foreground, to discard. There was a great deal of cross-checking. Throughout, I had the great benefit of being able to consult a Sanskrit scholar, Simon Brodbeck of Cardiff University, deeply familiar with the *Mahabharata*, who put me right at a number of points!

The work took eight, slightly interrupted, years, and the finished book is about 850 pages long. There is an apparatus that makes it easy to navigate – chapter summaries, a glossary, and an introduction and afterword.

Apart from its being a compelling story, a number of aspects of the epic interested me particularly. To mention only two – unusually for an ancient epic, the female characters have plenty to say for themselves, and actively influence events. None of them is told to stop talking and go to her room, as Penelope is told by her son in the *Odyssey*. True, one of them has to become a man in order to achieve her life's ambition, but she is an exception. The epic brings out very clearly the influence that women can have, as well as the great suffering that war inflicts on them.

Second, I wanted my version to bring out the moral complexity that runs through the epic. Although bitter conflict is central, there is no simplistic division between heroes and villains. There is a central concern with dharma, the timeless question of what constitutes right conduct for a given person in specific circumstances. Resolving this question is no easy matter. No character is unequivocally good or bad. Even Duryodhana, the main 'villain', is scrupulous in his adherence to the warrior code. And Krishna, the divine avatar who sides with the heroic Pandavas, engages in a number of 'dirty tricks' in support of their cause.

The *Mahabharata* says of itself, with only a little exaggeration:

What is found in the poem I have recited [...]
may be found elsewhere. But anything
it does not contain will be found nowhere

and indeed, allowing for changes brought about by the passage of time, it is easy to be persuaded that this is true. In my version I tried to bring out something of the encyclopaedic and visionary range and depth of the original.

Carole Satyamurti, Mahabharata: A Modern Retelling, *W.W. Norton, $19.95, ISBN 9780393352498*

LEONARDO BOIX

from *Table Variations*

A Family Ceremony

And she laid the table
and she asked everyone to sit around
and she prayed with her eyes shut
and she thought we prayed with her
and he looked at her
and then looked at me looking at him
and warm blood overspilled the chopping board
and the knife went in
and I didn't want to see
and he said to me
don't be so gay, no seas maricón
and I looked at my empty plate
and pressed my hands under the table
and ate my words
and they tasted like burnt barbecue
and Mother thanked the Lord with her eyes shut
and we thanked the Lord after her

CLARA JANÉS, *translated by Louis Bourne*

No Truce

This is the crystal ball
that hides everything,
but you toss in the equation.
The cloud chamber's walls
will say something.
The little goats draw near.
I am as much a sphere as an angle,
and I will give you no truce.
Where is that rabbit
that knows all
by not knowing it?
A serpent
comes out of the sea,
comes out,
comes out of the sea.

The Dunes of Your Shoulders

The dance of hands
doesn't hold the blades of grass –
a thousand million angstroms, perhaps,
glazed by your eyelids.
The melody you don't know returns
with its unrelenting key.
Crowned with feathers appears
the square root of twenty-five
plus minus sixteen.
What does the dot mean
next to the fraction bar?
That's how you provoke me
so I bite
the dunes of your shoulders
and arrive through the jugular
at your marrow's most secret nook.
Toss me the Greek letter
and split me in two,
for the night owl shows no fear.

IAIN TWIDDY

The Needles

At home, waking amid the chalk-white walls,
the childhood bed that surrounded me then
like a boat floating me out into sleep,

the east light that the silver birch lapped in
like the first flaps of the rooks in the oaks
over the road delivering me home,

I think of the Isle of Wight, the Needles
like white tilted sails cutting the sea,
the sun sizzling at the crumbling cliffs,

a projection onto the skull's back wall,
a blanched patch not branded into the brain,
but the clear space left when all else has burned.

I wonder did we really take the boat
out to the lighthouse, the stick-of-rock stripes,
did we really wobble onto the dock,

touch the windy steps, the tins, the big bulb
that revolved like the sun around the earth,
earth the sun; or have I imagined it.

Either way, however close we were then,
dementia has smashed even that light out,
like every other lighthouse in the mind,

so no thought can reach its destination.
I lie back in the thinning waves of light,
before I hear her risen, or I see

the damage another night has brought in,
the eyes like lighthouse bulbs in the daytime,
the body the brain's massed waves have wrecked.

I wish they could just stop for a second,
just stop crushing in, smashing the rocks, just
shush, shush, give me one last morning to make out

her voice, like a soul overboard, calling out.

The Hearing Aid

She's dressed, yammering on about the battery,
on and on at my dad, distressed, 6 a.m.
It must need a new battery or something.

The hearing aid needs a new battery.
We'll have to put a new battery in.
Have you got the new battery?

Do you think it needs a new battery?
It needs a new battery, doesn't it.
Is there a new battery for it?

It probably needs a new battery.
Then, *Where's Dad? Has he got the new battery?*
Is he bringing the new battery?

She's about to go up again
when he comes down, and stands by her,
as she stands by him, watchful,

as he fits the tiddly, fiddly battery
– she wouldn't stand a chance by herself,
given her butterfly hands, her landslide mind –

and he fiddles with it a while until
the squealing clears,
the frequency smoothes,

and she looks up at him, my dad, wide-eyed,
and says *Thank you, Thank you,* she says,
Oh, thank you.

And it's a small mercy, I guess,
how dementia means I'll never get
to see her as a serene old lady;

but I will as a little girl, as a child
with her hand held out as if for a shell,
as if for the first time

wide-eyed and open-mouthed at how
this tiny thing could hold such immensity,
a bounty as boundless, say, as the sea.

HELEN MORT

Rain Twice

i. Rain in a headtorch

drifts sideways through the beam,
slicks across a lemon moon

and makes the woods a mystery
of dog-scent, winter mulch.

Pre-dawn, when Sharrow Vale
and Psalter Lane lie down to weep

proud as a grandmother
and not your grandmother

but mine – tears that never fall,
caught by the landscape of her face,

tears a lifted hand could wipe away
and so I raise mine to the silver trees

and pause and look and run again
until I run like horizontal rain, run

with just my failing light
and this false gravity.

ii. Night rain

Rain tiptoeing
on the roof
of your van
then quickening,

the way you say
I enter a room:
deer-like, tentative
then definite.

I can't stand
outside my body,
see myself
a shadow animal

against the wall
but I take
your word for it, lie
still on your chest

and find you
too beautiful
to look straight at
so I look at you

the way rain
touches the roof
a thousand times
lightly

trace your shoulder
the way drops
move down
the windowpane

and when you
turn to me, the rain
falls through
the night's thin skin

and my skin is less
than paper
so by now
I must be drowned

must be an envelope
soaked in warm water
held to the light
so you can

see right through me,
how I break
and make the world
seem solid.

MARY JEAN CHAN

The Fencer

History

At the age of thirteen, I wielded a blade because I had a firm grip, I was in love with Shakespeare, and the school team needed an épéeist. When my mother flew to Linz to watch me go 3–4 down she gripped the railing until her marriage ring was folded into skin. I wanted to melt my blade.

Strategy

You never duel against the same person, even if it is the same person. On the *piste*, once the blades are tilted upwards, you recalibrate to thwart their every move. She was disarmed by my tears, the sudden time out to breathe through the yellowing bruise on my pale, yellow skin.

Footwork

Changing into school uniform felt like cross-dressing. I took my time: removing *mask*, then *chest-guard*, lingering at the *breeches*. The day I learnt to *lunge* I began to walk differently, saw distance as a kind of desire. Once, my blade's tip gently touched her wrist: she said it was the perfect move.

Attack/Defence

My greatest weakness: the *riposte*. In the changing room, the girl I was about to duel said I smelled of bitter gourd. We were practising the *flèche* – inevitably, I collided with her – a blur of entangled blades. I glimpsed her expression through our masks' steel mesh: her gleaming, smiling upper lip.

Grip and Point Control

French/Pistol Grip: one offers stability, the other more room for surprise. Before I came out, I asked myself: *French/Pistol Grip?* Now, my lover says: *your endurance is amazing.* Thank years of hard work on *point control*: how two fingers manoeuvre the blade's tip – a flurry of sickle moons.

LIZ BERRY

Spiritualist Church

I've never spoken to anyone of this –
the Spiritualist church, its squat brick body,
the mossy wall where snails congregate
in worshipful hundreds on wet dusks.
Every day that first winter,
the winter I thought would bury us both,
I walked past that church in sallow light
carrying my son at my chest,
my bones luminous with tiredness.
I'd stand at the gates and read
the inscription on the sign
   Light Nature Truth
drawing it into my mouth like anaesthetic
until I believed it was a message for me
to ascend like a dove through the red roofs
or sow myself into the sod.
     When the snow fell
I thought it was snowing inside my body,
milk turning to ice in my breasts,
snow piling sullen in the crib
of my pelvis. The air burnt my lungs
and I was back on a trolley in the mint room,
frozen from the waist down,
certain he was dying, that I was letting him
die and they were cutting me open –
     When the sky was dolorous
with sleet, I stood at the gates and dreamt
of begging them to take us in,
to lift my baby from my arms
and lay me down in a room of shadows
so I could shut my eyes at last and the hush
would cover me like a burial sheet

and someone gentle would rest their palms on me,
touch me with a light so staggering
I'd be opened up, my soul rising
from the X-ray of my skeleton
like a white-veined moth, my body below
hollow as an instrument, humming
with voices: women in darkness,
women with babies, down on their knees
in smothering houses, standing
on bridges, coats loosened to wings,
all of them uttering, murmuring at once: *I see you.*
Now understand, that love can take this shape –
a dove plummeting through white-sleeved night,
that this is a healing, a laying on of hands.

Early

There are times we're like new sweethearts,
awake through the shining hours, close
as spoons in the polishing cloth of dawn,
or sombre winter mornings,
the terrace a diorama:
bare poplar, yellow window, a woman
rocking a baby in her arms.
I tell you things I've never told
another creature, strange lullabies
like the purling of larks, winging up
into the withdrawing dark.
In the early light
every line I wanted to write for you
seems already written, read
and forgotten

so I sing the secret part, my true one,
of being born again
as you were born,
of kissing your mouth in the hospital,
love-sick, cut, stitched, undone
and forgiving you for everything
your sweet love would thieve me of.

Placenta

Some women eat theirs but I buried mine
    beneath the black waters at Wren's Nest
with a steel shovel and my bare fingers
    delivered it back to the subterranean fires.
It was a gorgeous bloody thing   mechanical
    but carnal   veined like a beast's heart
it smeared my hands burgundy   my mouth
    with the starry gut-punch of our first kiss.
Blood oblation, the weight of it knocked
    the breath from me   and when I cradled it
above its grave it was crawling with jewels
    trilobites and brachiopods   blinking eyes
which saw only briny hot darkness and flood
    upon flashing flood of creation.
The land moaned as I knelt   parting her seams
    the chamber within soot and pearl.
I spoke his name and spat on the plot.

WAYNE HOLLOWAY-SMITH

[Extracts from Love]

Dad's dick

Floppy dog tongue
Pig's snout
Chip-shop sausage on Saturday afternoons
Lyric I of Sunday lunches
Meat protagonist
Centre of all narrative dénouement
Never read a book never cooked yourself
A meal
Switch on the oven O organiser of the family unit
Avid keeper of numbers
You're full to the brim with flinching
To the brim with nothing
Violence
Lifter of toilets seats
Maker of stains
Itcher
Nervous twitcher
Drunkard
Stitcher-up of mothers
Rest easy your work here is done

Swindon

Here's your mother she is sleeping dressed in ostentatious pink
in the passenger seat of a brown-beige Vauxhall Cavalier
   her hair done perfect curated   the windows done
up tight   the exhaust fumes are your father gently filling up the car

Patti

Here's your mother she is Patti Smith and gazes hungry
in November   in 1969   in Manhattan in the Horn and Hardart automat
   upon a sandwich   in a vending machine   behind its glass
   with one less dime in her hand than she needs
Suddenly your dad appears dressed as Allen Ginsberg
buys her the sandwich and now she has to sit
and listen to him talk   about Walt Whitman
   for the rest her life
but instead of talk about Walt Whitman
he is silent   they are both rotated 90 degrees to the left
   and instead of an automat
   there are only armchairs a carpeted living room a TV

Ghost

Here's your mother she is Demi Moore with short black hair
it's the early nineties she's not got much on
   sitting at her pottery wheel
The Righteous Brothers are singing about love
it might be raining outside and dark
   and she's getting pretty messy there in all that clay
you might think   you might expect at this moment
the well-toned the shirtless husband
to arrive behind her in tight black jeans
   but nothing
only the record spinning and the half-finished jar
lengthening on that wheel

VIDYAN RAVINTHIRAN

Mercy Invincibility

We're playing Super Mario. This level's
designed for one player and not two.
The quick-collapsing platforms mean one always falls.
But when he hits the spikes he starts to flash.
The plumber turns invincible as a firewalker.
A chance to extricate oneself. How often
have our lives known that brief
immunity – the crisis which emits
a stretch of ardent unreflective life?
It's afterwards that hurts. Time salts all wounds.
You come to realise: that really happened.
But first there's a quick flick of the stick
as you leap my glimmering sprite between the spikes
and urge me onwards through a wall of fire.

Conversation

Bleakly, there seem two options only.
Sat beside each other, we're both lonely.
The patriarch presides, speaking of economics.
Or like wildfire there glows, in that space
each soul immures, a ragged half of talk. A voice
whose sad ironic echo has neither gravity nor grace.
The rational daylight of the Ikea uplighter
gives way to the darkness of a silent disco.
We're dancing to our private music, when the
devices fail, and, limned by their glow,
all those silent flailing bodies look absurd. Mimics.
You gesture in that vacuum for another shot.
But we've fallen through the floor and off the grid
and your face tells me mine is dead.

MARTINA EVANS

Clinical Indications

Oh was shorthand for the chemical equation
C_2H_5Oh – ethanol meaning alcohol,
a tip-off from the doctor,
a coded message
to say drink was involved / the patient was drunk.
The radiographer far away
in a deserted X-ray department at night
had to watch out for the obstreperous.
It might have been shorthand for Irish
but how could they scare me when
I only had to lay my Cork accent
like a wand on their ears?
Once I puzzled over
a request form for a chest X-ray
that gave one word – Irish –
in the Clinical Indications box.
Was it a joke? Or working backwards,
shorthand for the drink or drunk
or look out
for the telltale fractures of the third metacarpal
from frustrated Paddies punching walls
for the bilateral healed rib fractures
of the older labouring immigrants
who got so plastered they fell down,
broke, healed and carried on,
the stigmata inside the coats
of their skin like the rays from
a sacred heart? Or did it mean
what I never understood?
That night, the young doctor
with the black moustache
too close to me at 2 a.m.,

his breath in my ear, whispering –
something has to be done about the Irish,
they're spreading TB, spitting it
on the floors in Kilburn.
I'm scanning another man's head
so I can't move away from
the smell of his Wotsits.
I look straight ahead while
through the microphone
on the other side of the glass
my voice echoes –
keep still, you're doing brilliant –
to Mr MacNamara, yards away,
terrified on a moving table.

HUGH McMILLAN

Mongrels

With Robert Burns a sex pest,
Irn-Bru diluted to prevent
seizures
and Greyfriars Bobby
exposed as a clever gang
of street dogs,
we must doubt even more
the props of our race

and ask whether vowels
and a confused grasp
of history
are the only things separating
we noisy people from
the wee noisy people down there.
Last night while spruces shook
beyond the window

I watched a woman singing
'Biodh an Deoch':
her voice was like the
sea you hear when young,
broken and beautiful with
yet to be defined sorrow.
Chunnacas bat' air an fhairge.

She could have been singing
from a dessert menu
and I curse the folk who
barred me from my mother's tongue,
mealy-mouthed red-faced
pointless folk,
like me.

Rummaging in a box on St Andrew's Day

Sometime in the black-and-white era,
a man clips a sheep by a dyke.
Behind him a thin strip of land
tapers to tall trees.
The sheep on the trestle table
shakes a thin flapper's leg
at sullen skies.
The dyke could be any dyke,
the thin strip of land any thin strip of land,

only he knows what is behind the camera,
where the road took his boots
that evening,
which huddle of houses,
which hearth, which bairns,
which bible.
He is smiling under a rakish cap.
I imagine he came home from the war,
likes a dram. Salt of the earth.

Scotland is guessing like this:
how we pack the space between what we believe
and what we don't want to.
We use old books,
old songs, old solidarities,
memories of the relatives we knew,
exclude wife-beaters and psychopaths,
gossips and closet sadists,

and from the remaining handful
we weave a story fit for
land and seascapes

so beautiful they hurt.
Tonight if my sore leg permits,
and the moon is full,
I will walk down the glen
to where my people are waiting.
They will turn their faces
to me and we will imagine
past times to come.

JAMES BYRNE

from *WITHDRAWALS*

4

At the end of it is rot.
You brush and brush but cannot clean yourself like the moon does.

For a day you are unable to speak without opening your mouth –

converse of morning light –

you are hot and fetid
as if trapped
inside
summer's greenhouse.

Outside   the wind in your head
mocks and pounds –

Who do you think will remember you?
I won't.   *I won't.*

7

Your letter is like receiving a complaint from a local lunatic.

Tone performed, I take my time to reply, withdraw a month,

then write –

I am with you everywhere [...] like your ideas of truth and lying.

But my voice is not on the radio's UFO show [...]

Next Christmas you must come to our house.

But you are not a guest [...] Family never guests.

From now on, in this oven, we will check each other for signs of spoiling.

9

Head rush. Shudder rush.

You say that modern life is *always* busy

                          all of the time.

       So busy this.

Disturbance of sea-swill. Beached kelp, strung up and knotted –

    the negotiating table spread out like evolutionary error.

You echo duty   friendship as opposition.

But I am your baby. I am your gingled yolk.

12

Toxinal, shadow-scarp, the neighbours won't touch me.

The no-name couple at Number 4
                                    all rote and remote.

The children depart in matching Land Rovers.

                One with their mother, the other
                            with the father –

                            bill-hooks for eyes.

What land travels through them when they sleep? (Do they
                                                    sleep?)

A flag in the back garden, as if this were a consulate. Not
                    the rutting yard of a local vigilante.

All nationalism is a form of extremism. And you, son,
            are my sheriff.

Send me a letter, delivered the old way –
                brick, lump of coal through the window –

                your ultimatums   bound with string.

PETER GIZZI

The Present Is Constant Elegy

Those years when I was alive, I lived the era of the fast car.

There were silhouettes in gold and royal blue, a half-light in tire marks across
a field – Times when the hollyhocks spoke.

There were weeds in a hopescape as in a painted backdrop there is also a face.

And then I found myself when the poem wanted me in pain writing this.

The sky was always there but useless – And what of the blue phlox, onstage and
morphing.

Chance blossoms so quickly, it's a wonder we recognize anything, wanting one
love to walk out of the ground.

Passion comes from a difficult world – I'm sick of twilight, when the light is
crushed, time unravels its string.

Along the way I discovered a voice, a sun-stroked path choked with old light,
a ray already blown.

Look at the world, its veil.

Sky Burial

The robin that lives in my yard
also lives in me. This is the interior,
while the state unwinds across
a vast expanse splitting the sky.
It is all of it and more;
these things were passages
of the light-born afternoon
cascading then expanding
like a flange around the day.
Yes, the day, staccato
in its azure and gold banner;
then one learns, as one learns
from twilight, how to look
through here, and not here, grinning.
The wisteria out my window
is waving, up, down, up,
it's so far away though, outside.
I'm in here where the word is opening.
There are distances, the whole
tonal range blooming,
clarity of attenuated looking,
a payload delivering meaningful dust.
It's a good day to die.

Report

THE EDGE OF THE LANGUAGE
Poetry and poets in Japan

Katrina Naomi

I travelled in Japan for six weeks in autumn 2017, with a grant from Arts Council England's artist's international development fund. I'd wanted to visit Japan since I was eight, when I did a school project on the country purely because I liked the design of the flag. I knew very little about Japan – I'd purposefully kept myself quite ignorant. I wanted to be surprised, to be filled with wonder, like a child, and to write in response to that wonder. I'll admit I was also ignorant about Japanese poetry. After asking colleagues for recommendations, I travelled with Shuntarō Tanikawa's *New Selected Poems* (Carcanet, 2015, trans. William I. Elliott and Kazuo Kawamura), *The Penguin Book of Japanese Verse* (Penguin, 1964, trans. Geoffrey Bownas and Anthony Thwaite), Matsuo Bashō's *The Narrow Road to the Deep North and Other Travel Sketches* (Penguin, 1966, trans. Nobuyuki Yuasa) and Jayne Joso's excellent Japanese-themed novel *My Falling Down House* (Seren, 2016). I also took a poem I've always loved, 'My Tea Ceremony' by Henri Cole (from *Cole's Middle Earth*, Farrar, Straus and Giroux, 2003). All great introductions, but I was seriously lacking in women's poetry.

I knew one poet in Japan (Hiroshi Tanuichi, more of whom later). I was joining a walking tour in the footsteps of Bashō and being hosted for three weeks by Prof. Michiyo Takano at Yamanashi Prefectural University (YPU) in Kofu. Otherwise I was on my own. This felt like a good balance. I wanted plenty of writing time but also to get to grips with Japanese poetry and to meet poets, which would be tricky with my virtually non-existent Japanese. Sasha Dugdale, former editor of *Modern Poetry in Translation*, recommended I contact Andy Houwen, a Tokyo-based translator and academic. Houwen was kind enough to meet me, a complete stranger, on my second day in Japan and showed me how to behave at a tea ceremony – i.e. it's fine to slurp but don't ask for more – and presented me with the anthology *Other Side River: Contemporary Japanese Women's Poetry* (Stone Bridge Press, 1995, vol. 2, ed. and trans. Leza Lowitz and Miyuki Aoyama). In this anthology, I found Hiromi Itō.

You know that Emily Dickinson quote: "If I feel physically as if the top of my head were taken off, I know that is poetry"? That's how discovering Itō's poem 'Killing Kanoko' was for me. When I find a poem that knocks me sideways, I usually contact the poet to say so. It doesn't matter if the poet responds or not, it's something I like to do. Itō responded, straight away. I asked if I might interview her – being in another country makes me bolder – she said yes, if I could get from Kofu to Tokyo that Friday, she was reading at a conference on gender and poetry at the International Christian University (ICU).

The university clearly has a lot more money than most in the UK. I recognised Itō – she was short, with long black hair, dark glasses, a black Western shirt, black jeans and DMs, and loads of energy. I also recognised her poem 'Killing Kanoko' – it didn't matter that she was performing in Japanese, there were the rhythms of it, and the repetition (the poem is full of repetition). She stomped around the ICU conference tables as she read or chanted. I was brimming with emotion – this was why I'd come to Japan, for an experience like this. I couldn't stop smiling. I was still slightly stunned at lunchtime from her performance. I was trying to eat inari (tofu snacks) as unobtrusively as I could with chopsticks when Itō pulled up a chair next to me. I needn't have been nervous about talking with her; she was full of questions and smiles.

This poetry reading was different to any that I've been to in that it was followed by a 'life counselling' session. I didn't know Itō was a famous advice columnist in Japan and the US. In a confiding tone, she said: "Some people don't know I'm a poet." She seemed quite delighted about this.

After lunch, everyone was given a slip of paper and encouraged to hand in a 'life counselling' query. No one had to give their name and I should clarify that this counselling had nothing to do with poetry (but then again maybe it had everything to do with poetry?). Her advice to people regarding problematic marriages or self-centred children was wonderful. I particularly liked the advice: "When you want to run away from something, then run away." Simple, eh? Her advice regarding overbearing parents? "Give them something to cry about." Tough love. I later found out she ran away from her parents as a young person. I decided to put in the question: "What other things should poets do beyond writing?" She nodded, thought for a moment and said: "Some poets dedicate themselves to language, like – what's the word? – martyrs. They're useless." She grinned. A woman who'd volunteered to interpret for me where needed whispered: "'Useless' is very important in Zen Buddhism." The answer, and the interpreter's aside, made me smile again. Itō added: "As a poet you have no life-balance at all. That's obvious."

After the 'life counselling' session, I interviewed Itō. Straight away, she said: "My problem is that I can't write any more poetry." She paused and added, "But is that a problem?" I don't think it is. She's busy writing a novel after the death of her partner, the British painter Harold Cohen. She told me: "Writing a novel is step by step, so that everyone knows what is happening. Poetry is like jumping." And she literally jumps, like a cat. "Poetry has no goal, something comes springing up, you're in another place and jumping on to the next place." I feel sure Itō's poetry will come springing back up. She seems irrepressible.

I asked about the poem, 'Killing Kanoko', which she wrote over thirty years ago. It presents quite a radical stance on motherhood, certainly for the time. My take is that it concerns postnatal depression. "I wasn't interested in people's reactions, I was too busy raising my kids. But yes, people did want to quote it or mention it, put it in anthologies [...] people criticised it. Japanese literary scholars said it was a new style of poetry." She recognised this at the time: "I thought so too, when I wrote it. I thought, 'Now, I've got it.'" She talked about the rhythm of the poem and the repetition; the line "Congratulations on your destruction" is repeated throughout this long poem. She told me: "I'd recently moved to Kyushu [the most south-western of Japan's main islands] and went to this great festival and there was all this repetition of rhythm there and chanting, so

I thought of that particular rhythm, I was very surprised by it."

It's a surprising poem. I wondered if it was an anti-patriarchy poem. "Hmm, was I interested in putting down patriarchy? It was more the situation of the mothers [motherhood]. Six months after Kanoko was born, a year after a memoir on my pregnancy, *Good Breast, Bad Breast*, and my editor said why don't you write about your pregnancy? So I wrote 'Kanoko'. It was very strong feminism. I was considered a new style of poet against the old style of motherhood."

I liked her humour. Before Itō performed 'Killing Kanoko' she told her audience: "I will read my masterpiece. I wrote it when I was twenty-eight. And the kid is still living, OK?" In the interview, she said: "I'm always asked if Kanoko is OK." She continued, proudly: "She became a musician. She was a very ferocious young woman, like me. She used the poem 'Killing Kanoko' to make her own music."

Itō stated that she was "disappointed with some of the poetry that's come after, it's careful, quiet". She felt she'd been "at the barricade [...] facing it all". Still, she confided: "I feel uncomfortable if people feel they understand me in my poetry, don't you?" I said, yes, I did. She told me she'd stopped writing for a while: "I was imitating my own style of poetry – all those short lines. I got bored. Why am I writing poetry?" She paused. "We don't get any money writing poetry but we want to observe the world. This is the edge of the language we have and we want to go further, somewhere the language never came. So yes, I'm a poet, I'm interested in language."

Itō is returning to Japan after living near San Diego. "Living in California was hard." She continued: "My language is Japanese. In the US, I'm suffocating, no air, as if I'm a fish." She smiled. "My audience is Japanese." She will be teaching at Waseda, one of Tokyo's most respected universities.

By this point we had wandered off the topic and were talking about 'home'. I asked if she was going to give up living on Kyushu, a place she obviously loved – she'd been telling me how important it was "to live with nature". I agreed, I'd been telling her about Cornwall, where I live. She said: "I will stay on in Kyushu and teach in Waseda. I will fly every week. I can't live in Tokyo. I use the excuse, 'My dog is waiting for me!'" She laughed. After the interview, we caught a bus to the station, chatting and eating sweets. She checked I was heading for the right train and gave me a hug, as if we'd known each other for years.

I also wanted to meet the poet Jane Joritz-Nakagawa. Joritz-Nakagawa was born in the US and has lived in Japan since 1989. She is finalising a project with theenk Books in the US, called *women : poetry : migration [an anthology]*, including work by fifty women writing outside the country of their birth. She is also preparing her forthcoming poetry collection << *terrain grammar* >>. We had exchanged emails before my visit. I was interested in the experimentalism in her work and what she might say about her own poetry and that of her adopted country. Unfortunately, neither of us could be in the same part of Japan at the same time, so we carried out the interview during my trip by correspondence.

I began by asking how she would describe her poetry: "That's a good question. Recently it's abstract and minimalist often, but now too I am doing relatively more lyrical pieces. I've often been told I combine the personal and socio-political well in my work. The influences are both eastern and western." I asked her why she came to Japan. I was interested in her influences and I suppose I was also wondering at my own motives for visiting Japan. She replied: "I wanted to improve my thinking, I wanted to grow in every way such as intellectually, spiritually, emotionally and so on. I thought that might be good both for me and my poetry."

And has it been good? "I think I've absolutely broadened myself. This is the best sort of diversity training you can have, to move to a country where things are done very differently and people act differently from what you are used to. Of course it needs to be repeated wherever you go [...] Having knowledge of more than one culture puts you at great advantage, I think."

The poets she admires in Japan include Kiriu Minashita and Kyong Mi Park. "But there are lots of great poets here. I also like a poet who died in the 1940s named Sakutaro Hagiwara." Of the poets writing in English in Japan, she offered Yoko Danno and Eric Selland (the latter is also a translator). Joritz-Nakagawa also mentioned the *Tokyo Poetry Journal*, which has a good following. The *Journal*'s editors organise slams and other events; it's definitely worth looking up if you're ever in Tokyo.

Joritz-Nakagawa doesn't consider herself "part of the Japanese poetry scene because I write in English for an audience that mostly doesn't live here". But in a modest fashion, she mentioned she also wrote poetry in Japanese: "I play with Japanese but my wordplay in English is very serious." There was a smiley emoticon after this comment.

I asked her how trends in Japanese poetry differ from those in the poetry of the US and elsewhere. "What I am aware of is a great eclecticism

[in Japan], often a merging of techniques from various places and eras."
She continued: "Of course Japanese poetry has a much longer history than
the US and perhaps overall many Japanese poets may be more aware of
western poets than the reverse? Sometimes the awareness can lead to a
blended style. On the other hand...many American poets [are] drawing
on more than one culture in their work."

I also travelled briefly to Kyoto to meet Hiroshi Taniuchi and the poetry
collective JUNPA – Japan Universal Poets Association. In many ways
JUNPA is like a Stanza group in the UK. The group meets regularly and
members share their poetry, but JUNPA also has a publishing arm. The
two founding members, Mariko Sumikura and Taniuchi (Taniuchi is one
of several young members of JUNPA), have performed internationally –
the latter most recently at Ledbury Poetry Festival and at an event in
Cornwall run by the poet Sally Crabtree. Taniuchi posts a daily haiku in
Japanese and English on Facebook. He also writes free verse, as in his first
collection, *Plus One Word to the World* (JUNPA, 2011).

I walked with Taniuchi to JUNPA's meeting place via a fabulous indoor
market – it reminded me of Brixton's c. 1990. JUNPA gather at an Edo
period (seventeenth-century) house – all tatami mats, paper walls and
sliding doors, looking onto a small square of garden with stunted, if not
quite bonsai, trees. After the all-important greetings, tea and delicious
mochi cakes – which I'm delighted to report are generally vegan – everyone
settled down to write haiku. I'm used to a lot of staring out the window
when I write. Here, people seemed to dash off a haiku while I was still
opening my notebook or munching another mochi. I felt very inadept;
the only haiku I could read out by the time everyone else had written
several was one I'd written the previous week. During my stay, I became
faster at writing haiku, if only to try to keep up.

Anthony Thwaite's first line in the introduction to *The Penguin Book of
Japanese Verse* states: "Poetry is in a real sense a living part of the culture
of Japan today." JUNPA were very open, and with Taniuchi interpreting,
I wanted to find out if this was true. How important is poetry to the
average person in Japan? Here are some of the JUNPA poets' responses:
Mariko Sumikura: "Generally, people think that poetry is difficult. On the
other hand, they enjoy composing haiku, senryu." Still, she added, "People
don't respect poetry very much." Kikumi Shimoda spoke for everyone
when she said: "It is important for me." Taniuchi had a bleaker, more
political, response: "It is not important. It is not necessary to live on." But

as in the UK, when terrible things happen, some turn to poetry. Chiyo Kitahara: "Poetry is not so important in daily life. But after the dreadful earthquakes, I realised poetry is very important to people to share feelings, to support the sufferers."

I asked if haiku is still practised regularly or whether it was seen as old fashioned? Again, Kitahara spoke for most of the poets in JUNPA when she said: "It is rather contemporary, I think. Haiku never falls out of use because of its simple rule." And what about free verse? Here there were some differences of opinion. Kitahara said that it was not "paid full attention" because people found it "subtle", but she was glad its popularity was rising. And for Kazuhiko (some people are known by only one name in Japan): "It is not possible to express poetry except via free verse."

Is poetry considered elitist? Most, like Kitahara, said that poetry wasn't considered important enough for that: "Poets are not regarded as influential people." Sumikura echoed this: "People do not respect [poetry] very much."

'Life counselling' sessions aside, there seem to be more similarities than differences between poetry in Japan and in the UK. After the JUNPA readings, we went for a meal and I was asked about Brexit and why the UK had taken this stance. It was hard to be balanced in my response. We agreed we needed more internationalism, not less. I went away with JUNPA's suggestions of poets I should read: Takashi Arima, Hakushu Kitahara, Misuzu Kaneko, Michio Mado, Kaoru Maruyama, Kenji Miyazawa, Etsuo Muka, Hosak Ozaki and Kazue Shinkawa. I sensed a real vibrancy to poets and poetry in Japan, and I have so much more to learn. I'd love to return, to "go further", as Itō puts it, towards "the edge of the language" and beyond.

GIFT BEARERS FROM THE SOUTH

The Moon on My Tongue: An Anthology of Māori Poetry in
English, *eds Reina Whaitiri, Robert Sullivan and Ben Styles,*
Arc, £11.99, ISBN 9781911469032

So Mayer on a new anthology of Māori poetry

. . .

Closing *The Moon on My Tongue* is a poem that brings home its
profound reach, underlining both the vivid perceptual and
linguistic flexion that British readers have been missing without access
to these Māori voices, and that they were here in the UK all along. Briar
Wood (Ngāpuhi), who studied at the University of Sussex, writes:

> Those of us living in London
> how we miss you [...]
> After years and years here kūmara
> some of us still worship you.
>
> ('Kūmara Hōu')

"Kūmara" is sweet potato, and the poem opens by invoking its ancient
journey from the Americas to Aotearoa, and ends by hoping its "wāina
tendrils – / [...] grow around the glowing globe". It is an extraordinarily
generous offering to the imperial metropolis of "purple jewelled" riches,

the perfect ending to the long ceremony by which the book invites readers onto its marae, its homeplace. That marae is both the collective Māori homeplace of Aotearoa (the Māori name for New Zealand), and the specific marae of the writers, who give their iwi (meaning "bone", an ancestral kinship group) in their headnotes. Many poems speak from and with responsibility to and between iwi and marae, interlinked.

To accept these poems' invitation is also to accept both the meaning of that responsibility, and that all non-Māori readers have a share in it: to rethink the colonial mindset that means this anthology stands shockingly alone as an Indigenous-edited poetry anthology published by a UK press for UK readers (Salt's excellent *Earthworks* series was primarily directed to North American readers) – while only three per cent of poetry and fiction published in Aotearoa is by Māori writers, who are fourteen per cent of the population. Even fewer Māori writers are known at all in the UK, predominantly novelists Witi Ihimaera (Te Aitanga-a-Māhaki) and Keri Hulme (Kāi Tahu, Kati Māmoe, Nordic, Celtic), whose poetry appears herein.

Ihimaera's powerful poem 'O Numi Tutelar' is subtitled 'At the British Museum, 25 June 1998', a reminder that Māori culture and history is inescapably part of British culture and history. Ihimaera is among "iwi Māori, gift bearers from the South", in one of many critical echoes of T.S. Eliot's 'The Journey of the Magi'. Come to bring news of many gods and to take back stolen goods, Ihimaera's choric speakers cry: "Make way, Britannia, Albion, Victoria Imperatrix, / make way our pūtātara are braying to bring down / your walls."

The glossary gives "pūtātara" as "conch shell". While the anthology is subtitled *Māori Poetry in English*, it is not only wildly, importantly macaronic, a poetic kōhanga reo (a "language nest", or initiative for elders to teach Te Reo in preschools), but also – as Joy Harjo (Muscogee [Creek]) and Gloria Bird (Spokane) title their essential anthology of Native American women's writing – necessarily a work of "reinventing the enemy's language".

The introduction, by Ben Styles, the editor for Arc's republication of the Auckland University Press edition (titled *Puna Wai Kōrero*), notes "a defiant refusal [in the poems] to explain away the nuances of the Māori", but it could equally be noted that the defiant use of Māori highlights a lack of relational and dimensional nuance in standard English. Thus speaking in the coloniser's tongue is, as J.C. Sturm (Taranaki iwi, Parihaka and Whakatōhea) says, 'A Tricky Business'. Sturm's poem, reminiscent of Brian Friel's great anti-colonial play *Translation*, commands:

Over that river:

> Not of Babylon –
> No-one sat down,
> Not the Rubicon –
> Some came back,
> Not the Styx – well
> Maybe for some.
> No, that river had
> Has a Taranaki
> Maori name

A stringent (and indeed astringent, given its narrow columns) reminder that the colonisation of New Zealand was violent, despite the national myth of a kinder imperialism, 'A Tricky Business' rings its changes on biblical, classical and British history with ease and cutting precision. The rules of standard English are reinvented across the line-break of "had / Has" – and in the withholding of the river's name.

This is not just poetry but diplomacy, true (and unacknowledged) legislation. As Leanne Betasamosake Simpson (Michi Saagiiig Nishnaabeg) details in *As We Have Always Done: Indigenous Freedom Through Radical Resistance* (2017), Indigenous communities have always practised internationalism, and several poems here touch on transnational Indigeneity, either through the mobility of references across multiple iwi, or poets with both Pasifika and Māori heritage, or moments of recognition. Hinemoana Baker (Ngāti Raukawa, Ngāti Toa Rangatira, Te Ātiawa, Ngāi Tahu, Germany, England) writes:

> It's not the fault of the game, says Peace. I draw the ferns
> in a chart alongside mucus and masturbation.
> I put down the books and say a prayer for concentration.
> That place online where you can listen
> to thousands of crickets slowed down and
> they sound like the Mormon Tabernacle Choir.
> Yes, and a Lakota soprano sings with them in Italian.
>   ('My Life Part II: I Think You're on Your Own with That One, Bro')

"Concentration" is the mot juste for the poem's focus and density, its cultural distillations and admixtures: rhyming with "masturbation", it brings the poem from scientific, Eurowestern registers of language to the place where body, spirit and world meet. Technology can only connect the Māori speaker to a Lakota singer through crickets.

Baker's first collection appeared in 2004; one of the anthology's original editors, Robert Sullivan (Ngāpuhi/Irish), who started publishing in 1990, writes in 'Waka 46', "oh to be in that generation / to write in freefall picking up the tools / our culture has given us" – a promise that Baker's work appears to bear out. It's noticeable that older poets often didn't publish until late in life: Pearl de Vere Boyed (Ngāpuhi, Ngāti Hine, Ngāti Te Ata and Ngāti Kahungunu iwi) was fifty-five when her first collection appeared in 1988. There are distinct generational shifts and markers here: a timeline would help narrate the movement from isolated 'firsts' towards critical mass. Although both Hulme and Ihimaera have achieved international success as novelists, it is clear that Hone Tuwhare (Ngāpuhi iwi – hapū Ngāti Korokoro, Ngāti Tautahi, Te Popoto and Te Uri-o-Hau) was the galvanising force of contemporary Māori poetry, publishing thirteen collections of poetry between 1964 and his death in 2008.

The anthology includes 'Rain-maker's Song for Whina', one of several poems that allows the reader to glimpse the complex outlines of contemporary Māori politics. In 1975, Whina Cooper "instigated the famous hīkoi [protest march] from Te Hāpua in the north to Wellington", and Tuwhare captures her in full flow. *"This is a sacred march,"* she announces, and closes her speech, *"Kare tenei hikoi oku, he hikoi / noa-aha ranei ki te miri-miri i nga paoro o Te Roringi"* – which cites the walk's purpose as "to caress the scrotum of Te Roringi" (the Māori name for then-Prime Minister Bill Rowling).

That intensely rich intimacy is evident in Tuwhare's description, in another poem, of struggling with writing under the pressure of speaking for and with Māori tradition:

[...] eye-ball

to eye-ball I share bad breath
with the flared nostrils of the night.
For it's not me I leave behind: not me.

('On a Theme by Hone Taiapa')

It's an image of the sleepless poet as old at least as Pangur Bán (Old Irish, ninth-century CE), given a visceral new specificity by its use of the hongi, the breath-to-breath ritual Māori greeting.

Tuwhare's place in the anthology is both as poet and honoured elder and ancestor: several headnotes remember his teaching, and there are two tribute poems: 'In Memory of: Hone Tuwhare' by Tania Hinehou Butcher (Te Arawa, Ngāti Raukawa, Tainui) and 'Elegy' by Tru Paraha (Ngāti Hineāmaru, Ngāti Kahu o Torongare, Ngāpuhi). It is both notable and not, within the context of the collection, that these are both by women. This is one of the most gender-equal anthologies extant, putting more august national projects to shame. It includes a number of poems that invoke the power of women, particularly older women, as teachers and leaders (and hot-tub users, in Ngāpuhi poet Marewa Glover's lovely 'Ngāwhā'). None are more powerful than 'Me Aro Koe Ki Te Hā O Hineahuone!' by Jacq Carter (Ngāti Awa, Ngāi Te Rangi, English and Irish), which offers a concentrated vision of mana wāhine (powerful women) both ancestral and living. Like Ihimaera's pūtātara, it sounds a warning against exploitation and offers a rallying cry for resistance:

> If Hinetītama
> can become Hine-nui-te-pō
>
> crushing
>
> the next man who tried to interfere with her
> between her thighs
>
> then I too can deal to any man
> that would enter me without my permission.

The moon on these tongues is illuminating, and blinding. Poetry in Englishes needs its light.

So Mayer's most recent collection is (O) (Arc, 2015). <jacked a kaddish> is forthcoming from Litmus, Autumn 2018.

RECLAIMED EXPERIENCE

Sophie Collins, Who Is Mary Sue?, *Faber, £10.99,*
ISBN 9780571346615
Lila Matsumoto, Urn and Drum, *Shearsman, £9.95,*
ISBN 9781848615687
A.K. Blakemore, Fondue, *Offord Road, £10*, ISBN 9781999930431

Alexa Winik discovers a powerful "poetics of vulnerability"

. . .

The thread that connects three new poetry collections – Sophie Collins's *Who Is Mary Sue?*, Lila Matsumoto's *Urn and Drum*, and A.K. Blakemore's *Fondue* – might be easily traced back to an earlier work: Anne Carson's 1992 essay 'The Gender of Sound'. "Let us dwell for a moment on this ancient female task of discharging unspeakable things on behalf of the city," Carson writes, "and on the structures that the city sets up to contain such speech". Analogous to cathartic ancient rituals, these collections together construct a hybrid and self-reflexive chorus of women's voices that unleash "unspeakable things" – from violent traumas to ineffable joys – through poetry that feels as inventive as it does important.

Out of the three collections, Collins's *Who Is Mary Sue?* is the most expansive in scope. Collins masterfully assembles a cross-section of critical discourse, journalistic pull-quotes, lyric essays, and experimental free verse to launch an urgent interrogation of the cultural conditions that continue to suppress women's voices, specifically in the aftermath of trauma. These hybrid poems are slippery in tone and don many masks, creating crucial distance between poet and speaker that allows Collins to delve into difficult subjects such as violence against women and internalised shame.

The book's central motif – the dismissive epithet "Mary Sue" – is a fascinating mediating device that Collins deploys to depict the role of cultural production in gendering acts of speech and silence. "Mary Sue", readers learn, is a term drawn from the world of fan fiction and refers to an archetypal female protagonist associated with "narcissism and/or wish fulfilment" ('Who Is Mary Sue?'). In a long prose sequence, Collins recontextualises this term, however, as a symptom for the "double standards of content" that relegate women's experiences to the "narrower", supposedly inferior space of the private sphere ('Who Is Mary Sue?'). Mary Sue, then, becomes a spectre in the background of Collins's first-person poems, invoking a crucial question about how these double standards bleed into women's daily lives: if invented female protagonists are not even believed, then how could women survivors of "unspeakable" traumas expect to be?

As Collins depicts it, when women internalise this question, traumatic memory cannot be externalised and festers as debilitating shame – a psychic wound that is "awful, the size of a disc, / and deep" ('The Engine'). Yet what makes this collection a much-needed work of stunning feminist complaint is that Collins's female protagonists create forays out from this wound and its attendant silences. Among the mysterious personas and surreal dreamscapes that Collins summons, women's voices demonstrate incredible agency to reclaim unspeakable terrain as a site of productive fury; they "blurt things out" ('A.S.'), they "initiate the flames into their small routines" ('Untitled'). At one point, a disintegrating construction scaffold, personified with feminine pronouns, breaks away from its church wall with a brutal fury and makes "an unbearable sound" ('Healers').

These exquisitely disobedient voices reverberate throughout the negative spaces and intentionally blank pages of *Who Is Mary Sue?*, lending a surprising poise and generosity to a debut collection. They also mark Collins as a poet with a prophetic edge, one who discharges unbearable sounds not on behalf of any city's patriarchal social structures but on behalf of other vulnerable voices who may need a guidebook for surviving them.

Lila Matsumoto's *Urn and Drum* shares with *Who Is Mary Sue?* an urgency to interrogate the politics of what is unspeakable. Matsumoto, however, channels her observations through a more microscopic lens on material culture and the world of objects. This playful yet weighty collation of block texts, photography, allegories, and vignettes excavate a full range of "unspeakable / loss + bliss" ('Levels of Cognizance') within the commonplace. As Matsumoto writes in the aphoristic prose sequence 'Soft Troika', her desire is to "Follow the everyday without privileging adoresome buildings".

Matsumoto's attentiveness to the secret lives of objects is textured and sensuous. Details like "self-help muesli" ('Princess of flexible bamboo scattering light') and "fleshy foam sleeves" ('Peaches') exemplify the kind of hyper-awareness that colours the setting of this collection in high-definition. Here, seemingly static objects might accrue new meanings against a backdrop of loss. A jar's lightness becomes "a contradiction to gravity's will" ('Jar') and fondant cake is "here for you" with a side of "grief bacon" ('Fondant Cake'). Even the more enigmatic passages in *Urn and Drum* work to draw attention towards the small, inviting readers to "look twice" at the external world "because it gives off a ridiculous amount of bloom!" ('Soft Troika').

For Matsumoto, such attention is not a simple platitude for mindfulness but an embodied feminist hermeneutic. *Urn and Drum* exudes this perspective through the sounds and shapes of its textured dioramas in which "objects aren't torpid" ('Soft Troika') but always mirror back the self's own mutable and shifting identities. Moreover, Matsumoto's feminist poetics do well to reclaim the domestic sphere from the realm of the unspeakable, granting it a newly invigorated lexicon without inadvertently recapitulating into essentialist views of femininity.

With this continual reclamation of natural and domestic spaces, Matsumoto's brief and vibrant poems are deceptively complex. By examining the potentialities in seemingly static objects, she ultimately reveals a rich spectrum of human vulnerability reflected, namely the daily unspeakable realities of death and unfulfilled desire, the urn and the drum. Her striking, self-reflexive poems offer readers a convincing portrait of renewed attention to the external world and what it means to ask of that world "[t]o what extent is it sustained by longing [...] [t]o what extent is that longing mine" ('Meteor').

While Collins and Matsumoto opt for a more mediated approach in their poetry, the crystalline and terse diction of A.K. Blakemore's *Fondue* largely bypasses these distancing devices. In fact, Blakemore plunges straight into the borderlands of cultural taboo where readers encounter, among poems about ugly cats and mermaids, "the fractal stream" of pornographic ejaculations ('prelude') and a speaker who feels newly born like a "maybug the morning of nuptial flight" ('sadism') after a night of BDSM play. Sublimating taboo into delightfully odd euphemisms or metaphors is something Blakemore does exceptionally well.

But this strategy, though imaginative, accomplishes more than mere wordplay. For Blakemore, this oscillation between shadow and light, transgression and conventionality, all play into a broader ethics of writing towards the obliteration of stigmas around "unspeakable things". With such an emphasis on linguistic destabilisation, it's not surprising that mouths, throats, teeth, and gums are often invoked throughout this work. "this is a poem about my mouth," Blakemore writes in the collection's titular poem, "with this mouth i will teach you what it means / to live // without fear of contaminants" ('fondue').

Blakemore lives up to this claim as the poems in *Fondue* are captivating in their fearlessness. In another departure from *Who Is Mary Sue?* and *Urn and Drum*, *Fondue*'s brave ethics of destigmatisation emerge most effectively through compression and economy. Indeed, some of the most stunning moments in this collection occur when a poem teases out its political implications within the drama of a single line. In 'samaritans', as one example, Blakemore creates a bait-and-switch using heavy enjambment:

> and i never saw the point in talking
> when truth
> is just a sharp thing you stand on in the night, with
>   bare feet –
> unrepeatable
> as a kiss you said
>
> was forced, you never wanted.

In its brilliantly evoked final lines, this poem pivots from risk of sentimentality towards the immanence of trauma in daily life for certain bodies.

'Samaritans' is but one of many poems whose linguistic leaps and dodges keep *Fondue*'s reader skipping along its darkly bewildering corridors. It also suggests a broader theme in this collection: that taboos might be reclaimed not just as fury or invigorated language, but also as revelry. For Blakemore, celebration seems to represent an embodied resistance to shame and loss. As the speaker admits to herself in 'dandelion', "you / have no very deep understanding of what / it means *to be human* // but you damn well know you've got to play".

Collins's, Matsumoto's, and Blakemore's varied poetic universes remind readers that to be human is to be endlessly contingent. Gender is, of course, one contingent point amongst many. But across these provocative and poignant collections, gender's social construction is the primary site where each one might refresh and reclaim the politics of "discharging unspeakable things" and advance a much-needed feminist-informed poetics of vulnerability. I have no doubt that readers who encounter even one of these books will feel, along with the speaker in the concluding lines of *Who Is Mary Sue?*, "seen, in some important sense" ('Postface').

Alexa Winik is completing an MA in Poetry at the University of St Andrews.

ALL HUMAN SCALE

Robin Robertson, The Long Take, *Picador, £14.99,*
ISBN 9781509846887
David Harsent, Salt, *Faber, £14.99, ISBN 9780571337859*

Kit Fan on connection and disconnection, hybridity and virtuosity

. . .

Of the numerous cinematic techniques at a director's disposal, few can match the breathtaking long take – Truffaut's last scene in *Les Quatre Cents Coups*, Hitchcock's masterful *Rope*, the Copacabana sequence in Scorsese's *Goodfellas*, and the seventeen-minute weightless, digital universe in Cuarón's *Gravity*. The long take emblematises cinematic virtuosity, but also pushes form, rhythm, narrative, space, and time to their limits. The same can be said of Robin Robertson's book-length filmic verse-fiction, an immersive, virtuosic long take focused on Walker, a D-Day veteran from Nova Scotia, who after fighting in France is exiled to the United States, spends a decade of his life drifting from New York to San Francisco and Los Angeles, and finds the country consumed by McCarthyism, racial violence, ruthless capitalism and urbanisation. Having seen *Deadly is the Female* in LA, Robertson's Walker is mesmerised by the "long take / inside the getaway car: one shot that lasted three minutes easy / and was just real life, right there". Superimposed over the melancholy and paranoia of film noir, *The Long Take* captures scene by scene the Sisyphean struggle of a mind-and-heart-broken man against the "monochrome world of the city", preoccupied by its rapid vertical and horizontal expansion, making us to wonder if "all human scale is lost".

The beauty of *The Long Take* lies in Robertson's seemingly effortless ability to evoke the magic of cinema on every page. Juxtaposing poetry with prose, dialogue with diary, flashback with the narrative present, Robertson has invented a hybrid genre liberated by its own hybridity, which breathes new air into the music of the English language, meticulously recording the numerous and luminous. Whether it is "*the kingfisher's flash, the coverts of a jay*" Walker recalls from the Nova Scotian landscape, or the corpse of a homeless person he encounters "with emptied pockets, / a rifled wallet and a scatter of photographs", or the vast metropolis with "the shadow building" "oblique and sharp as a guillotine blade", or horrors of war "*under the brief, dead light of a magnesium flare*" where he sees "*odd parodies of human beings*", Robertson's lines move with confidence and grace like "the granular / sheathing of a camera's leaf-shutter". These are by no means easy transitions in literary or cinematic terms – often changing geography, perspective, emotion, and time zone within the space of a page – yet the book thrives on the elliptical, moody, maze-like qualities that make film noir so seductive. Through the bewildering noise of demolition, freeway traffic, a movie car-chase, and gunshot-flashbacks, the book sings a coherent music that has a fine ring of truth and risk.

Reviewing it, John Banville wrote that *The Long Take* is "almost unbearably moving". It is tempting to remove Banville's adverb. Unbearability in the form of friendship beats at the heart of the book, especially that between Walker and his elusive friend Billy, a drug-addicted homeless black veteran. Their friendship provides a painful backdrop, including an unbearably heartbreaking moment involving the sharing of a secret Walker has kept since the war. Elsewhere in the book, walking alone through downtown LA one Christmas, Walker finds himself "making an inventory of loss" and confronting the demolished buildings. He writes in his diary: "citizens can either watch their own mortal decline, or see themselves outliving their cities. This is why I miss the island. Nature. We love nature because it dies, and then comes back to life. A resurrection we can believe in." Like an actor fully living in character, Robertson through Walker has created one of the most moving records in recent times of human fragility, ambition, injustice, violence, and our deeply troubled path through cities and nature. Its vision of destruction and loneliness recalls Sebald's *Austerlitz*; its ingenuity of form and style reminds us of Carson's *Autobiography of Red*; its sense of violence and the sheer joy and stupidity of everyday life evokes Murakami's *Kafka on the Shore*. Comparisons aside, however, *The Long Take* will be remembered for its unparalleled originality, and an uncompromising power of storytelling that transcends the boundaries of film, fiction and poetry.

Despite David Harsent's attention to light, passing of time, and the effect of turning a single page in terms of sound and sense in *Salt*, it would not do his new book justice to over-accentuate its filmic quality and compare it to a series of short cuts (usually only a few lines on a page) like the shower scene in Hitchcock's *Psycho*. For Harsent, visual vividness is a side-effect of sound, and *Salt*, in its fiercely understated form (what he calls "a ricochet of echoes"), is one of the most daringly inventive experiments with sound in contemporary poetry. "Ricochet" is an impactful, uncanny word and "echoes" imply repetitions of a past – both words suggesting an aftermath in which their sources are opaque, if not unidentifiable. This sense of quiet mystery flows through the book, as hinted by the epigraph from Antonio Pappano's discussion of the Tristan chord: "In the silence lies the secret." Equally illuminating is the second epigraph's comparison of Rembrandt with Rothko, and how their painting "bleeds to the edges". Silence, secrets and boundary-crossing might make an incongruous trio, yet in what Harsent has called the "common tone and mood" of the poems, *Salt* creates an eerily haunting, dream-like world that challenges our assumptions about poetic form and human connectedness. Reminiscent of Greek fragments or crystalline haikus, and as eclectic as "a moment re-remembered endlessly", the poems in *Salt* are simultaneously self-contained and interdependent. They capture the fiction and friction between music and silence, the concrete and the abstract, human separation and togetherness. They hum, in solo and unison, with a versatile, song-like quality that invites the accompaniment of musical instruments, like Heinrich Heine's poems rendered into song by composers across the centuries such as Schumann, Liszt, and Morton Feldman.

In an interview Harsent highlights the religious bearings of salt: "the intermittent mention of salt has to do [...] with its use as a means to excoriate, to the fact that it is one of the Sin Eater's ritual items (along with water and bread), that it is curative, and that it plays a crucial role in superstition." Indeed, salt, like gold, is one of our most culturally loaded minerals: it started wars and still saves lives; it draws the attention of deities and wards off evil. From the fifty-five different occurrences of "salt" in the book, Harsent symphonically captures our secular and spiritual, mineral and quotidian encounters with salt in myriad incarnations: "a line of salt, a jigger of salt at the threshold", "salt-flats", "salt-eaters", "a salted seam", "salt wind", "saltwater", "salt-wife", "salt-mist", "salt moon", "salt to the penitent", etc. Harsent in his Goldberg Variations on salt not only prompts us to question the protean flavour of this essential ingredient but invites us to experience the busy randomness and distilled stillness of lives being played out between an anonymous "she" and "he". Ben Wilkinson in his review of *Salt* focused on its unredeemably dark mood, but it should be remembered that the book also contains glimpses of unusual intimacy and unnerving beauty in lines such as: "Her spittle was wine and salt. Later, he took salt / from the tip of her breast with the tip of his tongue." In this sense *Salt* is deeply human, as "music is nothing more / than aide-memoire".

Despite their deceptively straightforward appearances, each poem, each line, and almost every turn of phrase in *Salt* creates palpitations and reverberations in the reader, as if "a single / word can unpick everything". "Be voiceless, / be still, leave yourself there lost to sound and sense", Harsent writes. In an age of poetry preoccupied with interpretation, *Salt* embodies a rare Zen-like confidence in our innate contradictions, seeking to "be always touchable" and "to go / touchless from place to place". *Salt* is indisputably Harsent's most inventive work, a truly remarkable book to ponder and savour.

Kit Fan's second collection, As Slow As Possible, *will be published by Arc this year and is a Poetry Book Society Recommendation for Autumn 2018.*

LOVE AND CONFLICT IN AN AGE OF DIFFERENCE

Li-Young Lee, The Undressing, *W.W. Norton, $25.95,*
ISBN 9780393065435
Faisal Mohyuddin, The Displaced Children of Displaced Children,
Eyewear, *£10.99*, ISBN 9781912477067

Jennifer Wong on history, salvation, exile and the articulation
of difference

. . .

In his latest collection, Li-Young Lee reveals a vision of humanity and
language stripped bare, as the individual searches for salvation. One
of the most celebrated contemporary Asian-American poets, Lee's earlier
works are often interpreted in light of his family history. Born in Indonesia
to Chinese refugees who eventually settled in America, Lee's maternal great-
grandfather was Yuan Shi-kai, the first president of the Republic of China.
Lee's father served as a Presbyterian minister in Pennsylvania. Together with
his family's experiences of exile and political struggle, such formative
experiences underlie Lee's questioning of love and conflict.

The Undressing revisits the theme of the beloved explored in Lee's first
collection, *The City in Which I Love You* (1990), but here he pushes
boundaries with the subjectivity of the lyric I, as he merges the identity

of the lover, the seer and the believer. In the title poem, 'The Undressing', the poet reveals a private, mystical, passionate world in which the sensuous and the glorious meet. The opening poem starts with a beckoning: "Listen." Recalling the amorous language in the Song of Songs, the body of the beloved in Lee's work is a place of refuge as well as consummation, a site where the individual assimilates the conflicts between spiritual beliefs and violence, between distrust and faith. Responding to the body of the beloved, the lover speaks:

> But all burning is not the same.
> Some fires kindle freedom.
> Some fires consolidate your bondage.
> Do you know the difference?
>
> ('The Undressing')

By pitting one kind of "burning" against another, the poet considers the gulf between cultures and races that culminates in "difference", as if such difference can be reconciled by listening and understanding. In my interview with him for *World Literature Today*, Lee explained his "allegiance to a logic of peace and a science of life" and how this concern is rooted in his writing.

The longer sequence, 'Our Secret Share', is a moving narrative of his childhood and growing up with conflict. Reflecting on the versions of society advocated by Lenin, Jefferson, Chairman Mao or Nietzsche in which hate and opposition seem inevitable, fragments of the speaker's family history return to him. He finds himself unable to face the loss of his sister who cannot cross the river in Indonesia to reach him on the other side ("And my sister remains balanced forever / in the air above the watery girl / upside down below her, / and she never dies"). The poet highlights witnessing history from a child's perspective, not understanding the suffering he has seen:

> Crouched on a ledge, undetected, I saw, through a neighbor's kitchen window, catty-cornered one floor below, their grandmother in a chair surrounded by angry students carrying wooden clubs, metal pipes, and kitchen knives.

Overcome by the impossibility of undoing these memories, the speaker seeks to reconcile the past, where one page reads hate ("*They hated us without a cause*") and the other page reads redemption ("*The fire had not harmed our bodies, / nor was a hair of our heads singed*"). In an article for the *New Yorker*, 'The Undressing: Poetry of Passion Laid Bare', Dan Chiasson points out that Lee's past as a refugee has become part of the "prehistory" in the poet's mind, while his best work "takes for granted a past of rupture and trauma, implying, beneath its placid verbal surfaces, the pain it seeks to transform".

In Lee's poetry, one glimpses the possibility of achieving a language of clarity and beauty, where the articulation of difference – racial difference being one – is the anchor, is subtext. In 'Reading, Counting, Playing Alone', for instance, the experience of otherness and longing for acceptance is embodied in the child's solitary play, where he is among, yet apart from, his peers: "And whatever God or disembodied companion he speaks to / is left outside the schoolroom door each morning, / to be met again later on the walk home by himself / along the railroad tracks [...]". Through such deeply lyrical and nuanced language, Lee portrays the loneliness and awkwardness of growing up as an immigrant, overcoming the risk of cliché and self-indulgence in writing 'identity poems'.

Faisal Mohyuddin's debut collection *The Displaced Children of Displaced Children* is an articulate and original book that explores the notion of truth, dream and refuge in history. Born to Pakistani immigrants and growing up in America, Mohyuddin embeds his narrative of cultural displacement with the influence of Sufi poetry.

The collection opens with a quote from the Pakistani poet-philosopher Allama Iqbal: "We have come to know our existence can never be erased, / Even though, for centuries, history has been our enemy". In Mohyuddin's world, memory becomes an act of love, revival and defiance against cultural or political erasure. Written in short sequences, 'Poems of Arab Andalusia' conjures a reimagined homeland, as the poet reflects on his identity as a son and at the same time a writer, dwelling on the dilemma of writing, an act that contains so much beauty and responsibility – "Our hands hold the words / of dead poets" – conscious that the voices of the elders and his family remain "in the latticed history / of our bones".

The first poem in the collection, 'The Opening', invites the reader to enter a profound, unsettling dialogue between father and child about the pain and blessedness of childbirth, and the salvation in forgiveness: "Father: When a surgeon / Saves your life by amputating a limb / housing a reservoir of poison, / You do not curse the violence".

In an interview with Dante Di Stefano, Mohyuddin admits that he feels "much more conscious of being seen as a 'Muslim' poet in a political sense" in post-Trump America. With an epigraph quoting a Muslim woman hoping to save other victims in the Westminster terrorist attack in 2017, 'In defense of monsters' is an outcry against the demonising of Islam in the name of anti-terrorism. Amplified by the choice of long, run-on lines, the poem protests against "our living hurt" and antagonism that arises from "the thin air of worry, towers of fear, / rejection, exclusion, law, and more and more cries for war [...]".

Central to Mohyuddin's work is the unavoidability of conflict. 'Ghazal for the Diaspora', from which the book takes its title, reflects on the rootlessness of those who have difficulty reconciling what they learn from a blood-stained history, embodied in that "swinging of an axe" and a chipped porcelain cup. Despite the threat of violence, there is the desire to be compassionate, to forgive, to receive people with openness and hospitality even if it means risking one's own safety: "wish peace upon every stranger who arrives at your door, even the thief". In 'Faisalabad', the poet questions the power in naming and renaming. Tracing the history of his motherland, Faisalabad, "the Manchester / of Pakistan", he revisits the deep wounds caused by imperialism: "the British were obsessed / with tangible things, like land and coin, / tea leaf and tongue, believed time / too could be colonized". Throughout the poem, however, music becomes the medium for love and healing.

While the poet's lyrical gift is evident in the longer, elegiac work that deals with the subject matter upfront, it is in his more subtle, succinct poems where his most assured voice lies, and where he engages the reader with new ways of reading history. For example, 'On the morning of November 9, 2016, I had an entire pumpkin pie for breakfast', in which the protagonist vents his anger against the newly elected president, is a powerful poem about the unequal relationship between the individual and the state, and one's troubled sense of allegiance to the nation(s). 'Song of myself as a tomorrow', inspired by Walt Whitman, allows the reader to experience how it feels to stand on the margins, to be misunderstood. Scattered with derogatory names, the organic shape of the poem evokes the tensions between self and world, while the individual – "despite the price of standing tall and free" – dares to carve out his own identity in America.

Jennifer Wong is currently completing a PhD on place and identity in contemporary Chinese poetry.

CYCLICAL THEORIES OF THE UNIVERSE

Hannah Sullivan, Three Poems, *Faber, £10.99,*
ISBN 9780571337675
Abigail Parry, Jinx, *Bloodaxe, £9.95, ISBN 9781780372341*
Phoebe Power, Shrines of Upper Austria, *Carcanet, £8.99,*
ISBN 9781784105341

Declan Ryan finds versatility, velocity and long perspectives in
three debut collections

. . .

Approaching a review of Hannah Sullivan's *Three Poems* in ordinary fashion is difficult: one almost wants to yelp, to plead for some special privilege, some bell or whistle. It's an extraordinary book, and Sullivan can – it seems – do just about anything; her language is fresh, at once contemporary, refined and razor-sharp; she draws unforgettable visual images which seem as easy as any ordinary sort of noticing, she rhymes if she wants to, unostentatiously, mischievously. The first of the three poems is 'You, Very Young in New York', a sort of 'Preludes'-era Eliot lit up on artisan cocktails. There is everything of city life in it, compacted into set-pieces, at times comic, at others poignant, and not only for their subject – the keening drag of young love, the "permeability / Of one person to another" – but its broader, atmospheric ache, a mood of "long perspectives" and of "infinity obscured by a bus". It can talk of Bowie and

Henry James and not feel it's doing either a disservice – it has the punchy late-night twitch of the pop song coupled with the elegant progressions of a sophisticated syntax.

There is narrative amid the snapshots, a novel in Polaroids, if you will, populated by proper nouns, by brands and the sort of namedropping that can be allusion or showing off, which feels suited to the 'Very Young' of its title, that kind of hectic library assemblage, cataloguing and discovery that mark out one's teens and twenties. It is made more gripping by being retrospective, odder by being in the second person – a known, knowing 'you' – and this sort of close but slant attention marks Sullivan out elsewhere too; at times it feels her project is to write down as much of the world as is possible, so it might be reconstructed. This is most explicit in the second of the poems, 'Repeat Until Time', which is obsessed with time, both in the small sense of "forever fumbling for the snooze button" and the larger, "Cyclical theories of the universe are out of fashion". This is a quieter, more meditative, denser poem but reveals itself to be no less witty, no less flashingly visual, balancing a tray holding negative capability and nuclear physics without making too much of a fuss about it, or forgetting to bring everything back to the seeable: "Universe after universe, each universe flat, / Consumed by fire, then cooling slowly, / Like ice cubes on August afternoons".

Somehow, the third poem, 'The Sandpit After Rain', is even better. It's a poem where "birth and death happen on adjacent wards", the narrator giving birth, her father dying. Again it's funny, "we agreed I had not been very brave", surprising, moving, at times breathtaking. I won't quote the end because its impact is heightened by being earned, but it's little short of magic. This is a book which uses fine detail and description to write about the grandest things, "*This is the world: / The street cleaning machine / The slow lob of rubbish / And the binmen calling*". Sullivan has found a way to write about a world containing Facebook, "hypnobirthing" and "authentic Mission dives", and somehow make it sing.

Abigail Parry's *Jinx* is a party in a bag – its biggest asset is its velocity. It's a book of charms, omens and card tricks, but hidden under the sleight-of-hand is a darker edge. Many of these poems are to do with wrong decisions, death-drive and addiction: the voices don't know what's good for them, or do and do the opposite anyway. It's highly musical – the opener 'Emma, you're a gamer' has something of Cole Porter to it, its withdrawals, and progressions – "Yes he's frank, but is he candid? Someone blundered / someone's bluffing, / and someone's slipped a joker in the pack." Parry has a great deal of control even when the poems freewheel or rebel, she can write a novel in a couplet, in 'Hare': "a virgin going down, / a widow coming back", or pull a twist ending, as in the loopily literal broken-hearted 'Arterial': "Anyway, I pulled off at Membury to write you this [...]".

She is thoroughly entertaining, in whatever form she tries on, and she tries on many. There are alter-egos, masks and characters, often winningly named – take a bow, The Amazing Geraldine – but Parry is just as adept at the seemingly personal, as in 'The Fossils in the Square and Compass', a poem about "marauding up the coast" which becomes something more touching as "The years lay down in layers" and "Our smiles are hard like flint". Parry's versatility means that some poems work better than others, but like a sketch show, if you're not happy there'll be something more to your taste along in a minute – it's hard to think of a reader who would fail to find much to enjoy, whatever their predilections, among this sort of toe-tapping variety show. Parry has a great ear – "The years are spent, and all your bitter sisters / shut your careless heart with rusting sutures" – and is an enthusiast, the dream host of this sort of abundance. Gamblers, conmen and shady types recur; an overarching moral seems to be, as in 'Spook and the Jewel Thief', "take care who you dance with, when you dance". Perhaps the most touching moment of deflated expectation comes in 'The Knife Game', a pointy allegory for adolescence that ends with an unequal rate of maturation – "Already, you know how to make a boy / do anything you want a boy to do. Already, I / know better than to play with girls like you."

Phoebe Power's *Shrines of Upper Austria* is a quieter, nervier sort of book, largely free of pyrotechnics, but there's a great deal of action taking place in its use of voice, in its hair-trigger reflexes. Power has a real knack for speech, not only in the poems in the reported, often ungrammatical and characterful English of an Austrian grandmother, but in less obviously vocalised lyrics, too. There are some brilliant things here, Power's deftness repaying rereading until her cadences are tuned into fully – 'fasching' and its chatty, swerving diction – "High loud music / wrenches in the outdoor light, rips fabric. Dance the children on" and 'Georgiana' with its deflating, perfectly pitched summation: "takes German class and speaks / fast with a curly accent she won't change. / She made today polenta, schweinfleisch, / and a salad, and does fitness". That "and does fitness" at once a punchline, an afterthought and a dig in the ribs. "She made today polenta" has a satisfying wrongness of a kind toyed with throughout, testing the reader's ear, a formal atonality to wrongfoot the Anglophone listener, mirroring a disjunction which is often its subject.

At times, Power strains a little in poems that announce themselves as bigger things, consciously reaching for gravity, whether in a prose poem sequence about a murder trial or another on climate change. Both are engaging, although 'Austrian Murder Case' peters out by not seeming to know if it's too long or too short, but Power's talent is best deployed in her apparently slighter, less set-piece moments. There is a thrilling, Nabokovian lilt to 'Name': "My grandmother's name was Chris. / ach ja – Christl. // a chrism, Christ with a lemon tongue" and a catching of easeful belonging in 'British' – "We walked the grounds of a club in Putney: bridge / over pond, black geese and a kind of moorhen". 'Rina' is another high point, its slow accretion of detail, its pacing, its analogies just so, leading to an ending full of understated feeling: "She didn't mention it. / Her eyes were just as big, / and bare, and blue as I remembered." Power's tone is spry, and perfectly suited to capture the fleeting, the momentary, as in 'Ice Rink': "this jolly light world / of flying and seeing; // the jolly bright world". She does this sort of painterly scene elsewhere too, including the title poem, and it makes for a book which creeps up on you, then lingers stealthily, its language off-centre and personable, "a zone of deaf white".

Declan Ryan's debut pamphlet was published in the Faber New Poets series in 2014.

THE DROWNED YEARS

Luljeta Lleshanaku, Negative Space, *trans. Ani Gjika, Bloodaxe,*
ISBN 9781780374123
Volker von Törne, Memorial to the Future, *trans. Jean Boase-Beier, Arc,*
ISBN 9781910345641

George Szirtes finds hope amid devastation in two recent
translations

. . .

The establishment of the Man Booker International Prize for translated fiction in 2016 markedly raised the profile of a number of foreign writers and their translators. There had been the Independent Foreign Fiction Prize before that but the Man Booker sounded a bigger gun. It is – and about time too – a game changer.

That is the story with fiction. Translated poetry, like any poetry, is less prominent but magazines such as *Modern Poetry in Translation*, now in its fifty-third year, and *Asymptote*, particularly, have given space to poems from a very wide range of languages, and publishers like Bloodaxe, Carcanet, Shearsman, and Arc, the latter most conspicuously, have consistently published poets from other languages, in Arc's case in bilingual editions.

The best known – possibly only internationally known – contemporary Albanian writer is the novelist Ismail Kadaré whose work emerged out of the totalitarian Communist period, chiefly under Enver Hoxha, and reflects conditions in that time. The leading Albanian poet of the next generation is Luljeta Lleshanaku, born in 1968. *Negative Space* is her second book in the UK, after *Haywire: New and Selected Poems* (Bloodaxe, 2011), though New Directions in the US have been publishing her poems since 2002. She is herself a child of totalitarianism and spent years under house arrest unable to publish her poems until the change of system in 1990.

Negative Space consists of selections from two recent books, *Almost Yesterday* (2012) and *Homo Antarcticus* (2015). The two books are different but witness to the same cinematic eye that registers the world in brilliant juxtaposed images, the whole built on a bedrock of erased history and personal experience. As she says in 'Small-town Stations',

> You don't forget small-town stations easily,
> the short stops with ordinary charm.
> If you pay attention to every detail,
> they will become our alibi for not arriving on time
> or for never arriving at all
> wherever we had set out to go.

But while her poems seem to be composed of small-town stations of material detail, under the detail lie the vanishings, as in 'Children of Morality':

> A door opened by accident.
> Light broke through by force
> and, as in a dark room,
> erased their silver bromide portraits
> which were once flesh and bone

The title poem of the whole book appears in the *Almost Yesterday* section. It is one of her longer pieces, consisting of eight parts, in which she begins with her own birth and traces history from that point, negative space by negative space. The Angel Gabriel appears to her and tells her to read "towards a galaxy already dead, non-existent / the kind of news that takes millions of years / to reach me".

That makes her work sound like a record of devastation but it is so full of life and vivid detail that it rings with hope and a revivifying ambition. The small stations with their fine detail are part of a far greater system, a cosmology that extends beyond Albania and the realm of autocrats. It is particularly in her long poems that it is displayed to us as a humane cosmology of understanding and apprehension.

'Homo Antarcticus', from the book of the same name, is essentially the story of Ernest Shackleton's 'right hand man' Frank Wild. It is, at one level, a study of masculinity in extremis, under conditions of ice, hunger, and hardship where "only a man chooses to break into the darkness of the mind / by conquering the body" and where the explorers' recipes from a recipe book rescued from a sinking ship are treated "as if these items were her lingerie". Here "[a] new language is like a fish: / first, you need to remove its spine / in order to chew it". The poem doesn't offer theories of masculinity: it offers a form of human life so you may chew on it, each scar of which "you could call indifferent and epic / and childlike".

'Water and Carbon', the other long poem, is a marvellous meditation on the value of the physical, on the purely materialist view of humanity. What is nakedness? What is it to attain physicality and then to transcend it? And then there is the tenderness, the sheer delicacy of things, as in 'Ageing':

Ask your mother what she knows about ageing.
Ask the elderly women of your family
lined up so beautifully
like silver cutlery in a cardboard box
waiting for a dinner that may never happen.

So we do ask. The translations, by Ani Gjika, follow that vivacious line and keep us moving with it.

Where Lleshanaku's way is to extend out from detail and to keep a discourse going, Volker von Törne (1934–1980) takes another route, that which was taken by some of the major post-war poets of Eastern and Central Europe: the way of such as Celan, Herbert, Holub, Popa and Szymborska. Disparate poets as they were, if anything united them it was the desire to concentrate, to dispense with superfluous rhetoric and description, and to work through symbols taken from everyday life. Personal experience was transmitted through fantasy or the inanimate. It was a Modernist revolt against the florid traditionalism of approved poetry.

Von Törne was the son of an SS unit commander but his own political commitment was actively to the left. He was keenly aware of Germany's

Holocaust legacy and dedicated himself to addressing it. That did not, in his case, lead to polemical poetry. As Jean Boase-Beier, his translator, says, he believed in the importance of critical and poetic distance. At that distance, with such compression, the material world becomes almost transparent and takes on a symbolic gravity. That means he can move from one level of reference, such as

> Come with me. The drowned years
> Are rising to the surface. Tonight
> By the river the fires
> Are burning again
>   ('Paths')

to a whole poem like 'What People Tell Me':

> Get yourself a fridge
> they tell me, to make sure your schnapps
> stays cool in the summer. Stock up on coke,
> they tell me, another winter
> is bound to come.
>
> They think quite simply
> of everything.

"Despair cannot save us", he writes in another poem, 'Free of my Fatherland'. Despair is what the poems are built from and on. But there are, at the same time, a few very beautiful and tender love poems. So 'Love Poem' begins:

> Black
> A cat
> On wind-soft paws
> The night comes over
> The roofs

Despite the "critical and personal distance" mentioned by Boase-Beier, the poems move us precisely by means of their sense of the personal. They are not sardonic remarks dropped by someone down the street or in a bar, they are small intense cries and confessions that refuse to put themselves at the centre of their concern. To Von Törne it is not so much that the personal is the political but the other way round. The political is his responsibility, not an extension of his psychic domain. And there is nothing dry or dogmatic about it, nor is it a wild-eyed sloganeering. It is disciplined to within an inch of its life. And that too is moving.

Even with the longer poems – and there is nothing here of Lleshanaku's length – it is a matter of joined brevities. There is no reminiscence, no presentation of the surfaces of the world as the kind of sensory physicality that powers Lleshanaku's 'Water and Carbon'. What there is instead is what David Wheatley, in his introduction, talks of as "a poetic map" and suggests its extent by reference to Catullus and Attila József. He thinks of Von Törne's poetry in terms of "heady and feverish pleasures". The pleasures are chiefly to be sensed in the commitment to implicit delights and to those points at which the discipline allows itself to breathe.

Although Von Törne died almost forty years ago, it is salutary to read him. Our world is becoming rather like his.

George Szirtes's most recent collection is Mapping the Delta *(Bloodaxe, 2016).*

NEEDY BABIES

Dorothea Lasky, Milk, *Wave, $18,* ISBN 9781940696645
Emily Critchley, Ten Thousand Things, *Boiler House, £10,*
ISBN 9781911343172

Srishti Krishnamoorthy-Cavell on fluidity, the maternal and the
avant-garde

· · ·

The first poem in *Milk* opens with the virulent autonomy of blood.
Pulling back from a dystopian blood-flooding of space to the still,
numb centre of the woman's body, it acknowledges a traumatic
overflowing that strains temporality, stalls action and saturates the text
that is to follow. The title, 'A fierce and violent opening', issues both a
directive to read as well as a play on words, setting up the simultaneous
doubleness of the pregnant body the collection explores.

In many ways, this poem proposes the core binary that the collection
unpicks and conflates in discomfiting ways – of creative vs procreative
labour, the violence inherent in the shaping of this (re)productive economy,
and art as a strategy for recovery. Speech acts are reimagined as fluids; the
transgressive, leaky bodies of *Milk* write through their histories and selves
to produce new, broken forms of matter. Where this generative trauma is
conceptualised as being feminine work, there is a complex examination
of the affective responses that are deemed socially permissible:

When they propped me up
They said, oh, she's so strong
But I am not
I cry too
I cried for you
You left me, always, in the rain

Lasky looks at how compulsory courage in the face of loss is a socially mediated performance that cuts against the private self.

The exploration of the body itself is textured – it is a function of loss, a seeping, weeping carrier of meaning, a site of artistic labour. For Lasky, the body is a visceral testimony to change and resistance. Her evocation of fluids – milk, blood, ejaculate – mackles the foreground of the poetic text that is concerned with similarly uncontainable, elemental performative utterances. In 'A hospital room', the segue to the traumatic interlude of a previous miscarriage is borne out through the physical act of walking. Throughout, this sentiment of "[m]orning walking is like a hospital room" bristles against the various ways in which the body imprisons through pregnancy and childbirth, swollen with language and longing. Later, this will painfully twin with 'A miscarriage', where the detached navigation of empty space is performed through free verse, turning the visceral body into a distant object and unexplored territory.

One of the best poems in *Milk* is 'The clog', which provides an unnervingly intimate audience with coagulating bodies and their tremendous resistance to relief by interpretation or expulsion. The familiar form of comforting milk is turned inside out – "Nipples hard with liquid or falsities / White and soft / I can't get it out". Lasky's bodies here are occupied with matter and liquid, they fracture under critical duress, yielding objects that are cruel in their unknowability. There is a failure of language in evacuating speech and emptying bodies, and in the desperate, tragic attempt to undo loss, it generates an ever-present, inescapable absence.

However, for a collection that is so invested in the question of fluidity and spilling over, including the formal refusal to use punctuation, *Milk* suffers from the inability to escape arbitrarily normative verse structures, such as the consistent use of capitalisation at the beginning of each line or the unquestioning investment in the personal pronoun. In some poems, such as 'Floral pattern', this partial commitment to untreated lyric language ("I feel super needy today / The worst part of admitting this / Is that no one will care") seems particularly oblivious of the artifice of form, relying entirely on an insipid transparency of language to communicate an arguably profound emotional response. Where the text triumphs, however, is when Lasky weaponises the entangling of parodic detachment with searing anxiety in poems like 'The Miscarriage', producing a dark, dry humour that sticks like burrs.

Throughout the collection, milk remains the evidence of a painful trace language, a faded script that connects life to its plenitude and possibility, and that persists beyond the shadow of death as grotesque, incontrovertible testimony: "Goodbye milk / Hello love / Nice to meet you tiny faucet / Hello milk / No / Goodbye milk / Goodbye life / Hello life / Goodbye hello / Death" ('Milking the rest of it'). Particularly poignantly, in poems such as 'Milk, No. 2', the maternal body is imagined as a glasshouse, with transgressive fertility meeting fragility of both the container and the contained. Here, death proposes a hyper-real existence – this body is a compendium of memory, loss and desire marked by the doublespeak of blood, in its joy and terror, death and life. Milk becomes a not-object, defined only through a series of prismatic negations and losses. Ultimately, where it shines, *Milk* invests the maternal subjectivity too with this weight of not-ness where greening bodies meet diaphanous ghosts. It is a study in translucency and porosity, a private confessional that, at its best, resists and transgresses the demand for public performance and the tyranny of cultural expectation.

Emily Critchley's *Ten Thousand Things* interrogates similar anxieties about motherhood and female creative labour, scrutinising the ways in which religious, philosophical, civic and environmental discourses come to be gendered. This is a collection of vibrant experimental poems, featuring a rich and enabling intertextuality that deconstructs binaries, proposes complex and fractured genealogies, and attempts to facilitate a dialectic of knowledge and omission across some of the works of Martin Heidegger and Tao Te Ching, via the lens of contemporary literary and political feminism. While the major poem in the collection that crystallises these investigations is the eponymously titled 'Ten Thousand Things', the entire text is a terrain marked by echolocation. This takes the form of individual poems speaking to and across each other, referential addresses that are proposed and answered at different points of the text, and the sense of intratextual looking inward and intertextual looking outward that characterises the limits of Critchley's poetics. This is a critical exploration of the private and public implications of poetic labour, its strident political scope and procreative burden.

The introductory piece, 'The Origin of the Woman in Art', is a prose-poetry-theory hybrid that speaks from under the shadow of a Heideggerian heritage, examining the object of women in art and women as art objects. "Precisely in great <u>women</u> (which is all we are concerned with here) the artist remains something inconsequential in comparison with the <u>woman</u> – almost like a passageway which, in the creative process, destroys itself for the sake of the coming forth of the <u>woman</u>." This dehiscence between the poet and woman is a matter of historical critical interest to Critchley. As a female avant-garde poet, she is part of a long tradition of feminist struggle within the movement for experimentalist women to be recognised for both their formal craft and their gender identity. In the first of many binaries that Critchley troubles in her work, the artist and the woman are excavated from underneath the signs of each other, rendering both visible simultaneously in resistance to a patriarchal order.

Tropes of the maternal flower across the text, invoked and deconstructed with tenderness, humour and vatic anxiety. One of the most sustained forms of this is Critchley's engagement with the ecofeminist ideal of the 'earth mother', the bristling bringing together of ravaged space and gendered body. Where she contemplates the scale of ecological destruction that human hubris has wrought, the poet offers a more complex entanglement of power relations instead. She writes in 'Something Wonderful Has Happened / It is Called You', ostensibly a private lyric act between a mother and her child, but one that reflects the longer arc of environmental collapse:

> It's not like I have forgotten
> how to worry
>
> – the disappearing forests
> vanishing species
> zone of sky above our heads –
>
> I pray that when you are older there may still be
> the forests, for instance, and the species

Where traditionally motherhood might be conceptualised solely as a function of generative labour and the corollary fear of being unable to protect the child, here we have the introduction of a more difficult temporal problem. This poem is perhaps best read alongside 'That Means You World (Part I)', where this fear reaches a tipping point in the irresolvability of this crisis "even if you have children / though you have your children's children / even you yourselves // (why is this self-slaughter / coming from)". Most critically, this temporal crisis of motherhood is its new inability to imagine a future. The domestic intertwines with the ecological unexpectedly, and the ground for a philosophical investigation that reads beyond the misogynist mastery of feminine nature is prepared.

'Hello Poem' is a tender lullaby to the creative process, and the engulfing bodies of poems and mothers enmeshed with each other: "Hello poem / You're such a needy baby // Hello poem / We play at silence games. You win" and closing with "Hello poem / You exist! You will! // Hello poem / Hello poem / Hello poem." This is a bringing into existence through an aching insistence, a refrain met with an absence of speaking back. This will later be remembered in 'Untitled (Fear Poem)' where the phrase "Dear baby, hello" talks back to the first interpellation but continues to stretch the ominous silence thin.

In an illuminating interview with Charlotte Newman on *Prac Crit*, Critchley discusses the complexity of feminist concerns that inform *Ten Thousand Things*. What particularly struck me was her discussion of the gendered responses to the line, a concept that at once demands a consideration of verse structure, moral boundaries (to stay within the lines of Eden, for instance) and the convolutions of lineage and heredity. Not just in its formal distressing of what lines might look like but in its iteration of boundaries, limits and systems, this collection then generates a rich investigation of spatiality – of ecopoetic home-making, unexpected domesticity, and the margins of the private, composite bodies comprising language, matter, base animality and the political signature of gender. This is a difficult but rewarding read.

Srishti Krishnamoorthy-Cavell is completing a doctorate in contemporary poetry at the University of Cambridge. She is a Ledbury Emerging Poetry Critic.

THE HALF-OPEN DOOR

Asha Lul Mohamud Yusuf, The Sea-Migrations, *trans. Clare Pollard, Said Jama Hussein and Maxamed Xasan 'Alto', Bloodaxe, £12,*
ISBN 9781780373980
Ana Blandiana, The Sun of Hereafter/Ebb of the Senses, *trans. Viorica Patea and Paul Scott Derrick, Bloodaxe, £12,*
ISBN 9781780373843
Cevat Çapan, The Voice of Water, *trans. Ruth Christie, Arc, £10.99,*
ISBN 9781910345672

Dzifa Benson finds wildness, ennui and valediction in three new translations

· · ·

Reading these three collections of poems in translation can't help but concentrate in the reader's mind the notion of faith. The fact that the three languages in question here are wildly divergent from each other complicates an exercise in what it means to place trust in the translation process. Questions abound, the most obvious being: how much is lost in translation? And indeed, how much is gained?

How can the reader be sure that the translator has chosen the best words in the best order? How much of the original has been edited to suit a British ear that is used to hearing poetry delivered in a peculiarly Anglocentric, lyric way? How much can the reader trust that the translator has inhabited and captured the tone and attitude of the source language? What happens to scansion, metaphor and allusion in these circumstances? Is it fair to compare and contrast the three books within the same short review? How does all of this sit vis-à-vis Paul Valéry's assertion that "all poetry is translation"? Should these things matter?

In short, how well-oiled are these machines made of translated words? The reader is never more aware of the limits – and by the same token, the boundlessness – of the English language than when reading a translation of poetry. For the most part, in these translations, the answers to these questions have to be taken on trust.

It's fascinating then to read a little of poet Clare Pollard's process, in her translation of Somalian poet Asha Lul Mohamud Yusuf's *The Sea-Migrations*. Pollard, who has had a long association and friendship with Yusuf, writes: "It was tempting to make Asha's work more palatable for an English audience – to be both translator and editor, knocking off the awkward edges. But instead I decided to damn fashion. It would be ridiculous to tidy and tame such powerful poems. I just had to look outside the mainstream lyric for models."

Yusuf's poetry is like a lot of other African poetry in that it strives for a communality at the heart of its orality rather than the individualism typical of mainstream lyric and western poetry. These poems, with their extreme alliteration and political rhetoric, need to be read with an attitude that doesn't equate an on-the-nose mode of expression and uncouched allusion as somehow lacking. Yusuf's wild poetry needs to be read and judged on its own terms because it highlights what can be learnt from a culture and poetry that emphasises a collective consciousness and one so radically different from the more buttoned-up, western style that aggrandises the cult of the individual. It also gives us a chance to engage with an aspect of Somalia that can't be culled from the headlines.

Although she has lived in exile in the UK for more than twenty-five years, is beloved across the worldwide Somali diaspora and has mastered the prestigious gabay poetic form that is usually the preserve of men, Yusuf is largely unknown to an English-speaking audience. *The Sea-Migrations* is her first full collection, a Somali–English bilingual publication. It is intriguing, exhilarating even, to read these poems in English with the equivalent in the source language on the facing page as a visual component to accompany them. Winner of an English PEN award, the collection presents a selection of Yusuf's poetry from the last decade.

The title poem is Yusuf's contribution to the Deeley poetic chain, which began in the 1970s to protest Mohamed Siad Barre's dictatorial rule. The Deeley poetic chain was started by Maxamed Ibraahim Warsame Hadraawi, considered by many to be the most significant Somali poet, when his political playwriting landed him in jail. Yusuf's poem further subverts tradition by declaiming from a woman's point of view, conflating the personal with the universal. Heavily alliterated on the letter D, which lends the poem in English a weighty authority, it bears witness to the privations and dislocation of Somali people all over the world:

All Africa has dilemmas, there are always disputes
but in this distressed continent, Somalis sink down to the bottom.
Their hearts only detest, they have rusted and deadened.
Love for their country's disappeared, they self-destruct.

Placed beside the Somali, it becomes clear how much Pollard has kept the spirit of alliteration without overwhelming the reader. It is also curious to note how the English is much more end-stopped and punctuated than the Somali:

Afrikaa dhib deris looga dhigay, daayin abidkoode
Soomaaliduna ka daran oo way, ugu dambeeysaaye
Qalbigaa intuu daxal ka galay, daamur wada yeeshey

In contrast to Yusuf's fiery but formally controlled poetry, that of Romanian poet Ana Blandiana in the two collections that combine to make up this new translation – *The Sun of Hereafter* and *Ebb of the Senses* – is stark, terse and so introspective it verges on solipsism, especially in the former. Blandiana is also a prominent political figure in Romania – on a par with Vaclav Havel in the Czech Republic – and won the European Poet of Freedom Prize in 2016. These collections mark a turning point in the poet's work, formerly a tool in the fight against totalitarianism, but now displaying a disillusioned ennui, or what Germans call *Weltschmerz* – the poet is the "animal / That devours itself with yearning" ('Illusion') – brought on by the lack of solidarity in the fight against a despotic government. It feels like a book-long lament exemplified by short, sharp jabs of pain: "My shipwrecked head at the shore / Like a star / With rays of thorns" ('Ships') – all of the poems in both collections are confined to a single page and many go no further than half a page.

Both Yusuf and Blandiana share an implicit preoccupation with injustice and an explicit study of the sea as a metaphorical device. Yusuf uses the sea to trace the mass migration of Somalis, while for Blandiana the sea is the poet's own body or psyche. She even goes as far as to say: "Nothing is so closely paired with / Me as the sea" ('Indian Ink').

These ruminations on the sea are also writ large in the work of the third and oldest of the three poets, Cevat Çapan from Turkey. But here, in his latest translation, *The Voice of Water*, the sea is the site and conduit of memory. Of the three poets, Çapan's musing on his themes – which encompass the natural world, friends and family, history repeating itself and colour – are the least opaque, rendered in folktales, story and music, especially birdsong and even Bessie Smith's blues. The poems are also the most rangy and expansive of the three translations, simultaneously timeless and supremely aware of and engaged with the passage of time – so much so that the poet says, "It gives me memories I never had." Çapan is a man looking back on his life acutely aware that he has more years behind him than ahead of him. There is something ancient and allusive in many of the poems, where the past is contemporaneous with the present, but interestingly, this continuum of time almost never projects into the future. In the poem 'Crete' for instance, political history, personal memory and images directly in front of the speaker meld different timelines. There is something valedictory about the poems too. The poem 'Alaturka' begins: "Here we are in a waiting room / at sunset / a handful of people who don't know each other" and closes with these lines: "Suddenly through the half-open door / Death sticks his head / and with his most seductive smile / asks to be one of us."

Circling back to the questions that opened this review, it is tempting to conclude that the translation of Çapan's book offers the most authentically rendered facsimile of the work. Çapan himself has translated several works from English into Turkish and vice versa and instinctively, Ruth Christie's translation of his work feels the most surefooted of the three.

Dzifa Benson is a poet, dramatist and performance artist based in London.

THE PANGS OF JOAN MURRAY

Joan Murray, Drafts, Fragments and Poems: The Complete Poetry,
ed. Farnoosh Fathi, NYRB Poets, $16, ISBN 9781681371825

Amy Key takes a voyage through the oeuvre of a rediscovered poet

. . .

I t seems appropriate to start with a line from one of Murray's own poems:

> There's a small tale I'd like to tell you here. A bit sad I believe.
>   Not too sad!

because the story is a bit of a sad one. Murray was born in London in 1917 to Canadian parents. When she was eleven she became ill with rheumatic fever, an illness which left her heart damaged. She suffered recurring attacks, nearly dying in her early teens, and this meant her life was one where rest was demanded of her. The writing collected in this book suggests that rest was ferociously resisted. She created a large body of work, including poems and plays, and these are collected for the first time here, along with drafts and fragments, following the discovery of her mythic lost manuscript in Smith College's archives. She died of congenital heart failure tragically young, at twenty-four.

Of all the things I identified with in Joan Murray's writing, the opening of this untitled poem was perhaps the most powerfully relatable:

> You talk of art of work of books
> Have ever sat down thought all that's to do
> That book to read that book to write
> Sat down stood up walked back and forth

I'd spent the past couple of months attempting to finish my second collection – making those micro-adjustments that seem to require vast planes of uninterrupted "writing time" to resolve. My vast planes of writing time were spent: scrolling through Twitter with a nausea I last felt as a child waiting for the timidity of Sundays to end; going wild about other people's poems; pulling up weeds (but leaving in the roots); finally tackling the hand-washing; pacing about desperate for my attention to be snagged on anything other than what I needed to do. It seemed to me that Joan got it.

Many other elements of her work appeal. It is full of pangs and I found it hard to get through a poem without finding something that would make me feel a little undone. 'The Builder' felt especially touching:

> Oh I want to wander over the hills and down to the water
> And if there is sea I want to pack it up to my arms
> And let the blue globe of all that water fill my mouth
> Rill up my head, my chest, burst out of the sullen seed of my loin.

The speaker seeks this consumption by the sea. In another untitled poem the speaker *becomes* the sea:

> Therefore I walk by women as the sea ponders by the shore
> I tremble and splash my spray by the cavern
> Hear my own strange breath and laughter
> But it is my echoing and I am unalterably the sea

I have a real weakness for women writing about the sea, abstracting the sea, swimming in the sea. In my own writing the sea is somehow the medium for the poems being there at all. I find myself asking: are we all swimming in the sea because it is a conductor for creating the 'real' self? The sea is ever altering; but it is unalterable in us:

O to what shame toward my own first cause,
I find that like both sea and air I am two things
Crystal and clear and at the other hand sweet mad.

It is probably this that most draws me to Murray's work; that and those
pangs I mentioned: "I am here with arms arms asking without voice / For
the stomach cannot always say something from the middle" – the pleading
in that repetition of "arms"! It reminds me of a song by the British riot
grrrl band Pussycat Trash – I was fifteen or so when I watched them
perform in a dingy pub in Sunderland. "My arms are stretching to be big
for you" they sang. It's the only scrap of their songs I have retained.
Murray's poem continues, "What to say what to say that only arms can
say it". I am extending my reach just thinking of it. The desire for physical
connection is palpable throughout, and I came to understand the sea
imagery as quasi-erotic (the "slavering of waves", "swaggering all sex wise
and opening the sky", its "profound surge"). This erotic tone can be found
throughout the collection, as in 'Sterility':

There was a night when women's breasts
Hung heaped above my sagging mouth,
And dripped their pure sensuousness like juice

and 'Fata Morgana':

To wander aimlessly
And to brush against...
Ah, to brush the edge
Of my skin
As I wander aimlessly

Words that might well leave "one panting / In their smooth voluptuousness".
Elsewhere the wind has a "melancholy chastity". I really admire this image-
making. Murray has a talent for blending a weird hotness with something
cool and possibly transcendent, bringing to mind Chloe Stopa-Hunt's
elusive and highly compressed work. Murray's "I have seen hills and
rhythm / Will not leave my head" ('Ascetic: Time Misplaced') made me
rush back to read Stopa-Hunt. It's not an image-for-image correlation,
more something in the feeling. See for example Stopa-Hunt's 'Painting

My Breasts', published in *tender* in 2016:

> Painting my breasts with
> Tulips, like the
> Dreadful things they are.
>
> This bounding old
> Heart held still,
> In a cup, in white hands

For me, Murray's poem 'Ego Alter Ego' states what is going on in both of their poetics: "As all small simplicities grow large / In voicing all so simply". I also enjoy Murray's spattering of compounds – "cherrycoloured", "mistressthoughts", "deepblossomed shecat" – and some slightly unhinged images: "slug trepidity", "smile beserkly", the sun "like a quick-sore running".

The collection includes some of Murray's letters, which I found fascinating for their lack of chit-chat or gossip. They are so wholly interior it's as though they're notes for poems or notes towards philosophy. I found myself wanting to lineate this excerpt:

> Like children we are always gazing out of window! In all my head there is no new thoughts. Where is this god who throws the very solar system out of gear for aspirant youth? I believe that is the basis for some stupidity...

Or to steal a fragment: "Here's the night spreading her knees so wide I've struck the moon and the first star".

I found it interesting to read her on being a writer. Searching for that mysterious feeling, which I can only describe as "poemy", she writes to her teacher Auden, "I have been trying hard to hit something of the spot in myself that produced the Eclogues". To a friend she writes, "I have all the multifarious demands of creation to battle against, the worst of which is a hideous perfectionist complex that kills everything cold." That feeling of isolation due to losing touch with what feels so elemental to the self: "The strangest sort of mood has finally collapsed upon me [...] Now I am utterly winded by the fact that I don't care a tinker's dam about reading or writing [...] or not dreaming, or not." In another letter, "It's so utterly bewildering to know just how to write decently somehow." I was mentally running a neon highlighter over that last phrase.

There's lots I admire about the "particular swimming" of Murray's thoughts, but even if in your reading you grant yourself the false comfort of "these were written in different times", I can't get over the use of racist language in a few of Murray's poems. For example, the "Mongoloid fool", in an untitled poem featuring a "creature of no-race" who nonetheless is "slit eyed" with a "saffron yellow seasick face". Or a poem loaded with a kind of white-middle-class sentimentality "in the voice of a young black boy". I wonder why this language wasn't acknowledged in the introduction or in other writing on Murray's work by Mark Ford and others. I asked myself why those poems were included. Then, to my shame, I realised I'd leapt first to erasure of the racist language (wouldn't it make me so much more comfortable not to know those poems were there!). I had to ask why we rescue from obscurity Joan Murray's work, when others who have been systematically excluded from publishing, from critical discourse, and from having the opportunity to be read for centuries, have not had such opportunity. In her introduction to this volume Farnoosh Fathi comments, "Murray belongs to a radical arc of American metaphysical women poets, most of whom still remain unsung". That, of course, is also true.

I'm cautious of valorising Joan for her early death and mythic route to rediscovery. When Auden selected her manuscript for the Yale Younger Poets series, publishing it some five years after she died, he said, "We are not publishing her poems out of charity, because she will never be able to write any more, but because they are good, and I hope the reader will approach her work just as objectively as if she were still alive." I'm glad for Fathi's faithful restoration of the poems, which in their earlier Yale edition had been "prepared for publication" by the editor – Grant Code, a family friend of Murray's – a process which flattened some of the more interesting and unusual elements of her style.

John Ashbery wrote that Murray is by definition a poet of "uncollectedness", of incompleteness. It seems to me that she captures a kind of exquisite isolation – a "distant majesty". A "ridiculous" letter to her friend Helen Anderson ends with, "It is splendid that you are so unalone". Somehow this new edition of her work ends Murray's isolation, makes her unalone with all of us who read it.

Amy Key's second collection, Isn't Forever, *has just been published by Bloodaxe.*

THE GEOFFREY DEARMER PRIZE 2017

Judge: Ocean Vuong

The *Poetry Review*'s Geoffrey Dearmer Prize 2017 is the first poetry prize I've judged in the UK, and I found the wealth of writing in this batch of poems so abundant, so wildly rich in styles and forms, that it was difficult to select the one winning poem without also acknowledging the many successful poems published this past year in *The Poetry Review*. So before delving into the winning piece, I'd like to highlight three honorable mentions that haunted me throughout the judging process: 'what my mother (a poet) might say' by Mary Jean Chan, 'from *WITCH*' by Rebecca Tamás, and 'Rapture Series' by Aria Aber. These poems range across languages, geography and time, and realize what we hope from poetry: they insist and make evident an innate yet seldom seen human multiplicity.

Among these poems, however, it was Raymond Antrobus's 'Sound Machine' that kept snagging me back to its emotionally textured and sonically charged wordscape. The poem gyrates through interrogations of grief and ancestry twinned with a brooded meditation on masculinity and selfhood, the gifts and burdens we inherit, despite ourselves, from our fathers. Hewn through the intersection of race, class, the canonical and the alternative, and garnering with it echoes of Derek Walcott, Natalie Diaz and Yusef Komunyakaa (particularly the latter's 'My Father's Love Letters'), the poem is as much an ars poetica as it is a raison d'etre for one's very life – steeped in the essential question of how we choose our own paths without (completely) forsaking those who made us. At once stubbornly local and subtly expansive, the poem refuses to bathe the past in nostalgia – but instead revisits its epicenters from the contemporary present, creating a simultaneity that sears and concusses – in ways, it feels, only poetry can. "It isn't my fault," the speaker declares in a voice given him by a father who *blows fuses*, "the things he made could be undone so easily". One of those things being, above all, a son – one who speaks, has spoken, despite the muted lexicons of complicated and unforgiving tongues.

Ocean Vuong is the author of Night Sky With Exit Wounds *(Cape), winner of the 2017 T.S. Eliot Prize.*

RAYMOND ANTROBUS

Sound Machine

My mirth can laugh and talk, but cannot sing;
My grief finds harmonies in everything
   – James Thompson

And what comes out if it isn't the wires
dad welds to his homemade sound system
which I accidently knock loose
while he is recording Talk-Over dubs, killing
the bass, flattening the mood and his muses
making dad blow his fuses and beat me.
It wasn't my fault, the things he made
could be undone so easily –
and we would keep losing connection.
But I praise my dad's mechanical hands –
even though he couldn't fix my deafness
I channel him. My sound system plays
on Father's Day in Manor Park Cemetery
where I find his grave, and for the first time
see his middle name *Osbert*, derived from Old English
meaning *God*, and *Bright*. Which may have
been a way to bleach him, darkest
of his five brothers, the only one sent away
from the country to live uptown
with his light skin aunt. She protected him
from police who didn't believe he belonged
unless they heard his English,
which was smooth as some uptown roads.
His aunt loved him and taught him
to recite Wordsworth and Coleridge – rhythms
that wouldn't save him. He would become
Rasta and never tell a soul about the name
that undid his blackness. It is his grave
that tells me the name his black
body, even in death, could not move or mute.

After Reading Ted Hughes's 'Deaf School' by the Mississippi River

No one wise calls the river *unaware* or *simple pools,*
no one wise says it *lacks a dimension,* no one wise
says its body is *removed from the vibration of air.*

The river is a quiet breath-taker, gargling mud.
In comparison, Ted is *monkey-nimble,*
fish-tremulous and *sudden.*

Ted is *alert* and *simple.*
Ted *lacked a subtle wavering aura of sound*
and responses to Sound.

Ted lived through his eyes. But Eye the colossal
currents from the bridge. Eye riverboats
ghosting a geography of fog.

Mississippi means *Big River,* named by French colonisers.
The natives laughed at their arrogant maps,
conquering wind and marking mist.

The mouth of the river laughs: a man
in a wetsuit emerges, pulls misty goggles over his head,
couldn't see a thing he breathes heavily, *my face was in darkness.*

No one heard him, the river drowned him out.

Raymond Antrobus *is a Hackney-born British Jamaican poet, educator, editor and curator of the Chill Pill event series. His pamphlet,* To Sweeten Bitter *(2017), is published by Out-Spoken Press and his forthcoming debut,* The Perseverance *(2018) will be published by Penned in the Margins in October. He is a Complete Works III fellow and one of the world's first recipients of an MA in Spoken Word education (Goldsmiths, University of London). He is also one of three current recipients of the Jerwood Compton Poetry Fellowship.*

His poem, 'Sound Machine', was first published in The Poetry Review, *107:1, Spring 2017.*

The Geoffrey Dearmer Prize *is awarded annually to the best poem in* The Poetry Review *by a poet who had not, at the time their work appeared, published a collection. It is funded through the generosity of the Dearmer family in honour of the poet Geoffrey Dearmer, who was a member of* The Poetry Society.

CONTRIBUTORS

Rachael Allen's debut collection will appear from Faber in 2019 • **Andre Bagoo**'s latest book, *The City of Dreadful Night*, is published by Prote(s)xt • **Khairani Barokka** is the author of *Rope* (Nine Arches, 2017) and *Indigenous Species* (Tilted Axis, 2016) • **Liz Berry**'s new pamphlet is *The Republic of Motherhood* (Chatto, 2018). The title poem is shortlisted for the Forward Prize for Best Single Poem • **A.K. Blakemore** is the author of two full-length collections, *Humbert Summer* (Eyewear, 2015) and *Fondue* (Offord Road, 2018) • **Louis Bourne** is a poet and Professor Emeritus of Spanish at Georgia College & State University • **Leonardo Boix** is a Complete Works Fellow and co-director of Invisible Presence, a development scheme to nurture new Latino voices in the UK • **James Byrne**'s recent collections are *White Coins* (Arc, 2015) and *Everything Broken Up Dances* (Tupelo, 2015) • **Mary Jean Chan** is a poet and editor from Hong Kong. Her debut collection is forthcoming from Faber in 2019 • **Jenna Clake**'s debut collection, *Fortune Cookie*, is published by Eyewear • **Sophie Collins**, author of *Who Is Mary Sue?* (Faber, 2018), is an Assistant Professor at Durham University • **Heather Christle** is the author of four poetry collections, most recently *Heliopause* (Wesleyan, 2015) • **Martina Evans** is the author of eleven books of poetry and prose • **Peter Gizzi**'s most recent book is *Archeophonics* (Wesleyan, 2016), a finalist for the 2016 National Book Award • **Wayne Holloway-Smith** is the author of *Alarum* (Bloodaxe, 2017) • **Clara Janés**, born in Barcelona, is a poet, translator, novelist and essayist, and member of the Spanish Royal Academy • **Hagiwara Kyojiro** (1899–1938) was a radical Japanese anarchist and DADA poet • **Karen Leeder**'s translations of Ulrike Almut Sandig's *Thick of it* won a PEN Heim award in 2016 and will appear with Seagull in Summer 2018 • **Hugh McMillan** is a poet from Penpont in Dumfries and Galloway • **Helen Mort** has published two poetry collections with Chatto & Windus, *Division Street* (2013) and *No Map Could Show Them* (2016) • **Katrina Naomi**'s latest collection is *The Way the Crocodile Taught Me* (Seren, 2016) • **Anita Pati** is from the north-west and is working towards her first poetry collection • **Anzhelina Polonskaya** was born in Malakhovka, a small town near Moscow. Formerly an ice dancer, she is the author of eight collections in Russian • **Richard Price**'s latest collection is *Moon for Sale* (Carcanet, 2017) • **Mel Pryor**'s collection *Small Nuclear Family* was published by Eyewear in 2015 • **Sho Sugita** is the translator of *Spiral Staircase: Collected Poems of Hirato Renkichi* (Ugly Duckling Presse, 2017) and author of *Native Genius* (The Elephants, 2018) • **Vidyan Ravinthiran** is the author of *Grun-tu-molani* (Bloodaxe, 2014) and *Elizabeth Bishop's Prosaic* (Bucknell UP, 2015) • **Róisín Tierney**'s pamphlet, *Dream Endings* (Rack Press) won the 2012 Michael Marks Pamphlet Award. Her debut collection is *The Spanish-Italian Border* (Arc 2014) • **Iain Twiddy** has written two studies of contemporary poetry • **Ulrike Almut Sandig** was born in 1979 and lives in Berlin. She has published four collections of poetry in German • **Carole Satyamurti** has published several collections with Bloodaxe. Her translation of the *Mahabharata* won the Roehampton Poetry Prize • **Andrew Wachtel** is Professor of the Humanities at Northwestern University • **Hugo Williams**'s most recent collection is *I Knew the Bride* (Faber, 2014).

Permissions: The translations of Ulrike Almut Sandig's poems appear with the permission of her publishers, and are taken from her collection *ich bin ein Feld voller Raps, verstecke die Rehe und leuchte wie dreizehn Ölgemälde übereinandergelegt* (Schöffling and Co, 2016).

JEAN NICOLAS DE SURMONT

FROM VOCAL POETRY TO SONG

Towards a Theory of Song Objects

£ 18.00, ISBN 978-3-8382-1072-8
180 pages, Paperback

ibidem Available at your local
Press bookstore or amazon.co.uk

Towards a Theory of Song Objects can be a useful complement to reading more specialized works on vocal practices and has the advantage of asking relevant questions of method and of vocabulary.—Cyril Vettorato, Revue de littérature comparée

Although the song is often the subject of monographs, one of its forms remains insufficiently researched: the vocalised song, communicated to the spectator through performance. De Surmont proposes ways of research and analysis useful to musicians, musicologists, and literary critics alike.

The Poetry Review
Summer issue launch at The Poetry Café, London

Join us at a celebration of our Summer issue in the Poetry Café, when our readers, introduced by **Emily Berry**, will be **Raymond Antrobus**, **Liz Berry** and **Martina Evans**. With an exclusive short film by **Andre Bagoo**.

11 July 2018 • Readings at 7.30pm
Food & beverages available all day.

The Poetry Café, 22 Betterton Street
London WC2H 9BX
Nearest station: Covent Garden

Tickets are free but must be reserved in advance at marketing@poetrysociety.org.uk

THEPOETRYSOCIETY

New venue, even more exhibitors

Free Verse
The Poetry Book & Magazine Fair 2018

Presented by The Poetry Society in association with the Institute of English Studies at the School of Advanced Study, University of London

Sat 22 September 2018
11am–5pm + evening event

At Senate House,
University of London,
Malet St, London WC1E 7HU
Nearest tube: Russell Square

poetrybookfair.com

INSTITUTE OF ENGLISH STUDIES | SCHOOL OF ADVANCED STUDY UNIVERSITY OF LONDON

THEPOETRYSOCIETY

Need a website to showcase your work?

We design great websites at affordable prices. Easily edit the content yourself. Bespoke design, domain name, hosting arranged. All our sites adapt for all platforms and devices. We design websites for lots of authors and creatives – so you're sure of a sympathetic approach.

'Aerta has provided me with a clear, elegant and informative website, rapidly updated to order, and at a price a writer can afford.'
– Glyn Maxwell, poet & dramatist

'Quick to respond, diligent, imaginative - what more could you want in a webmaster?'
– John Harvey, poet & novelist

Email: johnbiggins@aerta.co.uk
or call 07976629435
www.aerta.co.uk/writers

THE
Poetry Review

Podcast series

In-depth discussion, diverse views – conversation and new poems from poets including Gillian Allnutt, Ishion Hutchinson, Jacob Polley, Simon Armitage and – just added – Fiona Benson.

Free to download • Find us on Soundcloud • Subscribe via iTunes

Sinead Morrissey

Zaffar Kunial

Wendy Cope

One of the most exciting and important literary festivals in England
Carol Ann Duffy

The best festival in the country
Andrew Motion

A brilliant festival, in a lovely town... an absolute must for anyone who believes in the importance of poetry'
The Idler

Ledbury Poetry Festival 2018 will welcome a host of poets and poetry lovers with confirmed names so far including: **Jackie Kay, Benjamin Zephaniah, Hollie McNish, Wendy Cope, Owen Sheers, Sinead Morrissey, Liz Berry** and **Jane Commane**. 2018 Festival Poet in Residence is **Zaffar Kunial**; his debut collection *Us* is published by Faber in July & he will curate individual events.

The Festival will have a strong international focus including events with US poets **Major Jackson** and **Linda Gregerson** and events with German poet **Jan Wagner** and Columbian poet **George Mario Angel Quintero**. Unshaken by Brexit, Versopolis, the innovative platform for emerging European poets will return and continue for a further four years, backed by funding from the EU Creative Europe Programme. Versopolis poets, **Michał Sobol, Kateryna Kalytko, Tomica Bajsić**, and **Lou Raoul** from across Europe will join three UK poets for a highlight event. The UK 2018 Versopolis poets are **Sasha Dugdale, Sandeep Parmar** and Welsh language poet **Mererid Hopwood**. Refugee Tales will present an event including **Patrick Gale**, whilst poet **Paul Henry** and singer-songwriter **Brian Briggs** (Stornoway) will perform their new poetry and musical collaboration *The Glass Aisle*.

Ledbury Poetry Festival 2018 will celebrate and showcase the poets connected with its programmes for new writers including: readings from the shortlist and winner of the Ledbury Forte Poetry Prize for second collections with **Sandeep Parmar, Judy Brown, Emma Hammond, Sam Riviere, John Clegg** and **John McCullough** plus a Ledbury Emerging Poetry Critics event, examining the representation of BAME writers in poetry reviewing and critical culture. The Festival will feature writing workshops and one to one mentoring opportunities, plus open mics and the Slam.

Follow us on Twitter @ledburyfest
or find us on Facebook

poetry-festival.co.uk

Supported using public funding by
ARTS COUNCIL ENGLAND

RETREAT

Poetry, Fiction, Memoirs,
Playwriting and Song Writing

Residential Courses and Retreats
Yorkshire Dales National Park

Our inspirational writers include:
Willy Russell, Fleur Adcock, Lemn Sissay, John Hegley, April De Angelis,
Ian McMillan, Gervase Phinn, Jo Bell, Ian Duhig, Kim Moore,
Malika Booker and Zoë Strachan...

www.thegarsdaleretreat.co.uk • tel: 01539 234 184

THE LONDON MAGAZINE
Est. 1732

Essay
Competition 2018

1st place: £500
| 2nd place: £300 | 3rd place: £200 |

Opens: July 1st
Closes: August 31st

for details, terms and entry visit
thelondonmagazine.org/competitions